MORE
THAN
ENOUGH

How One Family Cultivated a More Abundant Life

Through a Year of Practical Minimalism

MIRANDA ANDERSON

ISBN 978-1-950283-03-3 (Hardcover)
ISBN 978-1-950283-04-0 (eBook)
ISBN 978-1-950283-05-7 (Audio book)

Printed in the United States of America

Book design by Morgan Crockett | Firewire Creative
Edited by Stephanie Stahl

livefreecreative.co

For Dave, loving you is my favorite adventure.

. . . .

For Milo, Eliot, and Plum, for being
more than I hoped for and all I'll need.

TABLE OF CONTENTS

INTRODUCTION   IX

PROLOGUE   XVII

PART 1 — THE CHALLENGE

1 THE GUIDELINES   1
2 A BRIEF HISTORY OF CONSUMERISM   7
3 REDEFINING MINIMALISM   13

PART 2 — PRACTICAL MINIMALISM

4 MORE VS. ENOUGH   19
   Abundance Exercise   30

5 CULTIVATING GRATITUDE   33
   Gratitude Practice   40

6 THE POWER OF PATIENCE   45
   Waiting Chart   56

7 IMPERFECT MINIMALISM   59
   Should I Buy This? Flow Chart   67

PART 3 — LESS STUFF

8 LESS STUFF = MORE FOCUS   71
   Five Favorite Things Exercise   80

9 BUILDING COMMUNITY THROUGH BORROWING   83
   Interactive Borrowing List   91

10 CAPSULE WARDROBE AND
   UNNECESSARY DECISIONS   93
   Decision Elimination: Making Some Choices Habit   104

11 THE VALUE OF SPACE   107
   Create Space Exercise   116

PART 4 — MORE ADVENTURE

12 IT'S NOT ABOUT THE MONEY   119
   Save To Spend Exercise   126

13 GIVING AND RECEIVING GIFTS   129
   50 Gifts Of Experience   144

14 CREATIVITY IN MINIMALISM   147
   Create Something   156

15 SELF CARE VS. RETAIL THERAPY   159
   20 Replacements For Retail Therapy   167

16 TIME AND ENERGY AS RESOURCES   169
   Time + Energy Management Chart   178

17 A LIFE OF ADVENTURE   181
   The Live List Activity   190

EPILOGUE   195

ACKNOWLEDGMENTS   201

ABOUT THE AUTHOR   204

INTRODUCTION

Have you ever told yourself that a new pair of shoes will make you feel better? Or that a new computer will transform your ability to work harder? Do you believe that bigger homes, freshly decorated in the latest trends, indicate the great success of the owners? Do you ever long to travel the world, but instead, more often find yourself traveling the aisles of your nearest store? Went in for one thing, came out with twenty?

Do you sometimes look around your house, with its closets and cabinets filled with things, and still feel a little empty? Like there must be something more?

Yeah. Me too.

For years I lived a very happy life, quietly watching and

waiting for the time when true success and contentment would knock at the door. I did all the right things: I got married, graduated from college, got a good job, and had a few kids. My husband and I worked hard and saved so we could buy iPhones, build a beautiful house on a big lot, and fill it with all the lovely things our hearts desired. We included wood floors and open shelving and even Pinterest-worthy hanging hammocks that swayed just-so when you relaxed into the cords.

We followed the path that had been loudly proclaimed as the journey to the American Dream—minivan and Madewell high-waisted denim jeans included. We were achieving all the goals we'd set out to reach, but found something unexpected on the other side of success: an insatiable desire for more. More success. And buying more stuff.

I wasn't entirely ungrateful. I had moments of feeling blissful within my life, and if asked I would have said that overall things were pretty great. But that nagging for bigger and better was consistent. I was often setting my sights on goals or gain, then postponing my sense of real happiness until it was achieved.

· · · · ·

I wasn't alone in my feelings of inadequacy and impatience for success. It seemed like everywhere I looked people were struggling with the same problem. The same constant drive to have better in order to feel better. It seemed as if the mutual whole of society had agreed to chase more stuff. In fact, it also felt a little bit like a race. A race to perfection, power, acknowledgment, and achievement. A race that didn't seem to have a finish line at all.

A quick scroll through Instagram could verify that almost

everyone was shopping their feelings, and proving their worth by the perfection of their houses, wardrobes, vacations, or business success. Myself included.

We were all filling our homes with things, not for their inherent value, but for the value we assigned to them. The cool factor of that on-trend mid-century modern couch that is just unique enough no one else will have one. The story of success that a designer handbag tells—when in reality its function is the same as the regular old tote bag you already own.

Our stories about our possessions are as varied as our lives and backgrounds. But they are all just stories. We wear complex clothes of emotions, mixed with our upbringing, multiplied by the outside marketing, and steamed in social conditioning.

We acquire stuff, not for what it is or what it can do, but for what we believe it will reflect back onto us. How the latest pair of Nikes will change us. How a new iPad will improve us. No one is ever really buying a product, but buys how that product makes them feel.

But do we really need the new stuff to feel the feelings, and what are these feelings really about?

What stuff adds value for me in my life might be different than what stuff adds value for you in your life. The things you love are very likely different than what things I love. What you want to feel might be different than what I want to feel.

And so, it's not about the stuff, itself. This never-ending race is actually about feeling better or feeling period and not about having more.

But for me the beginning of this journey wasn't about freedom, gratitude, and feeling content—it was all about the things we owned. It was about the stuff filling my cabinets and cup-boards, stacked in bins in my garage, and tucked away in the closet. It was about the time and energy I was spending every day sorting, organizing, cleaning, and managing the stuff, and the space where it lived. It was about constantly wondering how, when, and where I should get more or different things.

In a world where most of my decisions seemed to revolve around our possessions, I needed a break. And one day, I decided to take one.

I woke up to the idea for The More Than Enough Stuff Challenge after years of small steps toward simplifying, and looking back, they seem laid out like a pathway leading me to the life I have today. A life full of opportunity and freedom. A life of less stuff, and more adventure. A life where I feel better than ever before.

One year, overwhelmed with small children and a large house and too many decisions to make with too little time, I decided to consolidate my wardrobe to a very edited collection of my very favorite things. I pulled everything out of my closet, tried it all on, purged eighty percent, and was left with a tidy forty-five pieces of clothing including tops, bottoms, dresses, and shoes that I could mix and match to make endless combinations. The time and energy I recovered by no longer asking myself "What should I wear today?" gave me confidence that outweighed the worry that friends would see me in the same outfit more than once.

Feeling encouraged to simplify, I next tackled my laundry and cleaning routines. Setting one day for each household chore and sticking to it. I was systematically reducing my stress by eliminating deliberation. On Thursdays I cleaned the floors, on Mondays I did the laundry. I was experimenting with a type of practical minimalism that involved not only thinking about my stuff, but really considering how I was spending my time and energy.

I tried on short challenges. One was a no spend month in which we didn't spend extra money on anything beyond regular groceries. Just to see what it felt like to be conscious with our money. Another was called the "Spring Fling" where my sister and I challenged each other to sort through and donate one hundred items in the thirty days of March. I think I had donated one hundred by day ten, which said a lot. At the time, my husband and I were living in a 900 square foot apartment. I have no idea where I had been stashing one hundred (plus) unnecessary items. But, there they were!

When the idea to stop shopping unnecessarily for an entire year tapped me on the shoulder, in the biggest experiment so far, it was not completely out of the blue. This minimalism experiment, what we named "The More Than Enough Stuff Challenge" (what I will refer to in the book as "The Challenge"), was not the first step in the pathway to a grateful, abundant life, nor has it been the last. It was the pivot.

This was the year where the fundamental culture of our family changed. The year my perspective shifted and I practiced living a more meaningful, fulfilling, and sustainable lifestyle. The year I could not just say, but truly believe, that what I had, and who I was, would always be more than enough.

. . . . .

The purpose of this book is not to convince you to become a minimalist, or to encourage a year of not shopping. However, I want to share the lessons that we learned during this pivotal time in our family's life. I hope to offer a unique perspective, a shared experience, and maybe some relatable insights that will give you a chance to think about your own life in a new way.

Our year-long experiment of not shopping was simply a framework for living some basic values in a more tangible manner. I believe we all want to live more abundantly. We all desire that feeling of connection and peace. The choices we make every day are all in hope that we fill our lives with joy—and the things we buy are often to serve the same purpose. To help us feel more worthy, happy, or successful.

I hope you find within these pages something of value to use in your own life. And as you do, I want you to feel confident enough to actually apply the lessons in a meaningful way.

The following chapters will share the perspective changes and ah-hah moments that led to our family culture shift and living more fully a life that we desire. I am not going to take you chronologically month-by-month, because the lessons we learned wove through the whole experience.

My intention with this book is to reflect back, distill down, and offer up the most meaningful lessons and insights from our year of practical minimalism. At the end of the year I no longer felt like I was experimenting with minimalism. I felt like I was living an entirely new life with a fundamentally fresh perspective.

I will share memories and stories both from The Challenge and from my life. I will explain some of the history of consumerism and why we have redefined minimalism for ourselves.

In parts two, three, and four, each chapter explores one principle and lesson we learned, and at the end of the chapter, I have included an activity for you to use to apply the principle to your own experience. As you do, you will be more aware and grateful of the abundance that surrounds you. You will feel more connected to your true desires for your life. You will begin to see how you already have and are more than enough.

Come along, let's get started!

PROLOGUE

t happened the first week of January. I was trying to make sense of the chaos happening behind closed doors of our home in Austin, Texas. I had been organizing, and uncovered stacks of unused stationery and handfuls of colored pencils. Three pairs of craft scissors were hiding beneath the pile of fabric pendants ready for the next celebration. I noticed a letter that had been incorrectly delivered to my house *two months* before.

I set aside the letter (so I would finally remember to walk it over to the neighbor) and I turned back to the clutter. Old kindergarten workbook pages, five Sharpie markers, a roll of blackboard vinyl that should have been installed in the very cupboards I was organizing. Bins of chalk and baskets of paper. And this was just the first cabinet.

All in all I recycled, donated, or otherwise disposed of four full garbage bags of stuff. It seemed impossible that quantity of stuff had even fit in four tall cabinets. Yet, there it was.

As I sorted, stacked, and purged, the thought kept hitting me: "We have so much stuff!"

The funny part was, before I opened my cupboards that day, I thought I was somewhat of a minimalist! I had never really enjoyed shopping just to shop, and our family of five had always lived on a sensible budget. At this point, my husband Dave and I had been married ten years, and we had already moved eight times. Each time we moved, we decluttered and organized as we packed up everything we owned.

We spent the first few years of our life together nestled into a cozy 400 square foot basement apartment in Salt Lake City, Utah. I finished nursing school while Dave waited to begin law school. He worked as a valet, parking cars in the freezing snow, to bring in enough income to pay rent and buy groceries. We lived a minimalist-by-necessity lifestyle then. With little space and little money, but loads of love!

The next few years were a blur of moving, first to Puerto Rico for an internship, then New Hampshire for law school. After one year of school and one baby, we packed up again, this time headed to Alexandria, Virginia where we found a modest two-bedroom apartment with lots of potential and lots of great friends. I worked part-time as a nurse and ran a small custom sewing business on the side while Dave lived between the classroom and library at George Washington Law School, occasionally making it home for dinner before heading back out to study for exams.

We lived the best we knew how with limited space, time, and money. I creatively designed our small apartment to function as a family-friendly play area, a creative sewing studio, and a hub for entertaining, all with quick changes of scenery. I could tuck toys into baskets and out of sight when I hosted game night or our annual New Year's Day brunches. My sharp scissors and pins folded easily into the sewing closet when the kids were playing in the living room.

I knew not to buy more than we needed, and was necessarily constrained by both space and budget. But that didn't stop me from thinking about all of the things I wanted. I would pore over catalogs and admire my favorite new furniture or clothing. My Pinterest boards were filled with photos of beautiful, spacious homes with natural light pouring through floor-to-ceiling windows and well-appointed furniture placed just-so.

I had done my best with our small apartment, painting walls, arranging and reupholstering furniture, adding personal touches that felt like home. I loved where we lived, and how we lived, and I was also excited to move on to the next chapter. What I felt like would be "real life" owning a home, having more money, more time, more flexibility to just buy things, rather than circling them in the catalogs.

That time had eventually come, when with two babies and one on the way we packed up once again. This time bound for Austin, Texas where we would build a big home on a big lot. Where we would buy new furniture—the kind we really wanted rather than the hand-me-downs we had been making work. Where we would never again need anything else, because we would have made it. Checked the boxes for success and live happily ever after.

. . . . .

But on this day, three years after we moved into our dream home in that quiet Austin suburb, I was surprised by the amount of stuff we owned, and also weighed down by it. I had been pulling unused and forgotten items out of the cupboards for an hour when I felt something shift a little bit within me. A crack in my perception of what success looked like and what it truly meant to have enough.

Since moving to Texas with a bigger home, I had started shopping a little more. Feeling some flexibility and freedom. Ironically, I had also started being more aware of the excess that existed both in my own life and in the world at large. A blogger who I followed and admired had recently released a book that resonated with me. In her memoir *Chasing Slow*, Erin Loechner had quoted Epicurus: "Do not spoil what you have by desiring what you have not; remember that what you now have was once among the things you only hoped for." In moments I could humbly look around and recognize everything we had as all that we had ever wanted. I asked myself, "Can all we have now be enough?"

Another book that was helping me shift my mindset surrounding my lifestyle was *Essentialism*, by Greg McKeown. As a natural-born busybody, I was always up to my elbows in projects, goals, and tasks I had taken on. I had been particularly touched by Greg's emphatic declaration that choosing fewer, more meaningful activities led to a higher contribution and more fulfilling life.

> "The way of the Essentialist means living by design, not by default. Instead of making choices reactively, the Essentialist

deliberately distinguishes the vital few from the trivial many, eliminates the nonessentials, and then removes obstacles so the essential things have clear, smooth passage. In other words, Essentialism is a disciplined, systematic approach for determining where our highest point of contribution lies, then making execution of those things almost effortless."

These ideas of living a more meaningful life through focusing, rather than expanding my choices floated around in my head like balloons bouncing lightly on the ceiling of a birthday party. The seeds of prospective change had been planted, and with every additional stack and basket of unnecessary junk I pulled from my cabinets, I felt the roots start to sprout. Digging a little bit deeper.

. . . . .

Later that week, my interest still piqued by how to deal with all of our unnecessary stuff, Dave and I sat down to watch a documentary on minimalism. While the film shared a few ideas that resonated with me, a lot of the scenarios portrayed in the documentary were un-relatable and I had a hard time seeing myself in that minimalist world.

The stories that stole the spotlight were of wealthy, single men quitting their high-paying jobs to live out of a suitcase and travel the world. It was a cool idea in the abstract, but completely unrealistic for this wife and mom of three. I had a family, a house, a husband with a great job, and, for as much as we loved to travel, the nomadic lifestyle was not a good fit for us. Plus, I love throw pillows, potted plants, and a garden in my backyard. We could definitely trim things down a bit but living out of a suitcase was going too far!

Not all was lost, however. Two principles from the film jumped out at me, echoing the lessons I had heard in the books I was reading. Reminding me of things I already knew and truly believed. These were two things I could use and apply to my own, very normal life:

1. USE WHAT YOU HAVE.

2. KEEP ONLY THE THINGS THAT ADD VALUE TO YOUR LIFE.

That I could do. And as I was telling Dave that these were my takeaways, I was struck by an idea.

What better way to focus on using the stuff we already had, than by not buying any more?

I had just confirmed through my cabinet deep dive that we definitely had amassed enough office supplies. And a quick mental walk-through of the rest of the house confirmed we also had enough clothes, shoes, furniture, art, kitchen accoutrements, sporting equipment, books, and everything else I could possibly conceive of us needing in our day-to-day existence.

"What if we stop buying more stuff?" I asked Dave.

He looked at me with interest and asked me to explain further. He could already see my eyes sparkling with excitement.

"I mean, do you think we could not buy anything this whole year? Of course, we will need groceries and printer ink and consumable things. But, we have so much, and I can't imagine needing more!" Dave nodded with a big smile.

Now my head was spinning. I had that buzzy energy that comes when you're hit by a sudden, exciting, and somewhat wild idea. It was the first week of January, and I hadn't yet come up with my yearly resolution that would challenge and inspire me. Maybe this was it! Not buying unnecessary things would not only help us use what we already had, but also encourage even more gratitude and patience as we pressed pause on any random new things that we might want.

"The year just began. We can look at it as a family challenge. An experiment. What do you say?"

Dave was all in.

He usually is, which is one of the reasons we are such a good match. I have lots of crazy ideas, and he supports me in all of them. And as most good ideas usually are, it was a quick, easy decision without overthinking of all the reasons it couldn't work.

So, it was decided. We would work out the specifics over the next few days (and make a couple last-minute impulse buys: an instant pot and a Dolly Parton Vibes tee shirt. You know, the essentials.) And we were on our way!

I shared about The Challenge with the readers of my blog, livefreecreative.co, and I closed with the following exclamation:

"Cheers to a year of abundance and gratitude!"

And that is what it turned out to be, and so much more.

. . . . .

Over the twelve months of The Challenge, we did our best to eliminate unnecessary and mindless consumption, and more importantly, we developed a family culture of gratitude, contentment, and recognizing abundance in our everyday life. With the elimination of more, new things, we were able to really deepen our appreciation for everything we already had. Stepping off of the race for more, we found that right where we were was a really great place to be.

We navigated holidays without giving material gifts, resisted relentless social pressure to buy new and better, made lifestyle changes that eliminated unnecessary decisions, like deleting email subscriptions that enticed shopping, and only going to the store once a week for groceries, and our family grew closer than ever before. We spent our time and money on experiences and adventures, opting for weekend camping trips and visits to local museums with the kids, rather than acquiring more stuff.

Of course, we were not perfect, and had to make adjustments along the way to accommodate some unexpected life circumstances. For example, Dave taking a new job midway through the year and us choosing to relocate our family from Austin, Texas to Richmond, Virginia.

In the middle of our experiment, helped by the new job and relocation, we took the challenge a step further and downsized from our 2400 square foot house in Texas to a 1000 square foot temporary rental home in Virginia where we could learn even more about living well with less.

Through all of our months during our year of not buying things, using what we had, and living in abundance, I learned firsthand that life is bigger and more beautiful than anything we could ever need. My eyes became trained to focus on here and now, rather than if and when. I remembered that I am in the driver's seat of my own life, and I get to choose to be happy today, because I already have everything I could ever need.

I felt I had more than enough. Chances are, you do too.

PART ONE

THE CHALLENGE

"
Use it up,
wear it out,
make it do,
or do without.

Chapter 1

THE GUIDELINES

The purpose of The More Than Enough Stuff Challenge was never to stop shopping forever. Rather, we wanted to stop mindless shopping and reset our relationship with the things we already own. We wanted to cultivate qualities that would enable a more sustainable, intentional lifestyle that would continue even after The Challenge was over. But most people who learned about The Challenge mentioned that they would never last, or that the idea seemed a little too intense for their families.

They also had a hundred questions: What did you buy and not buy? What about shoes? Don't your kids grow? What about holidays? How did you do it? What did you miss the most? How much money do you think you saved? Are you crazy? Did the experience even make a difference?

We had some of these answers at the beginning, but for the most part we just took one day at a time, focusing on the present, and made adjustments as necessary. This was something we needed to do for us, to see what changes might come of this experience.

Just as convincing others to join The Challenge was not part of the plan, the purpose of this book is not to encourage you to begin your own no-buying challenge (although you may find value in trying something like that!). This book will also share lessons and principles learned along the way that have added a richness and perspective to our life, and hopefully they will help you too.

. . . . .

Below are the guidelines for The Challenge that we developed in the beginning of the year:

1. WE WILL NOT BUY NON-CONSUMABLE GOODS.
   ▷ Non-consumable goods were things like clothing, shoes, art and decoration, furniture and linens, books, accessories, technology, sporting equipment, toys, and basically anything I had brought home from Target or other stores in the previous six months. (The Dollar Spot is so hard to resist!)

2. WE WILL ONLY BUY CONSUMABLE GOODS AS NECESSARY.
   ▷ Consumable goods were things that are normally used up to completion like groceries, soap, printer

paper, batteries, and (as it turned out) my kids' socks that slowly disappeared as the weeks went by.

3. WHEN CONFRONTED WITH SOMETHING WE WANTED OR NEEDED, WE WILL EITHER:

    ▷ make it using supplies we already had on hand at home;

    ▷ borrow it from a friend, family member, library, or another lending service; or

    ▷ be patient and wait until the year was up.

· · · · ·

I should note here that I am a craft and DIY enthusiast. At the time we began this experiment, I had an in-home studio filled with supplies for making almost anything. In fact, when I told my good friend and neighbor across the street about our plan, she challenged me to make a lamp using all supplies I had on hand. I didn't end up needing to make a new lamp, but did confirm it would have been possible.

Throughout my life I had heard the old adage: "Use it up, wear it out, make it do, or do without." The Challenge felt like a true application of that idea. We would start to use up what we had and do without what we didn't.

When we started The Challenge, we lived in Texas where the mild weather meant we had a virtually seasonless wardrobe. So I planned on the kids being able to make it through the year without new clothes. My two boys, Milo and Eliot, love to wear sports clothing that is loose and stretchy, which meant their clothes did not become too small too quickly. My daughter, Plum, the youngest, wears dresses every day (and often a crown as well). So having her grow out of her clothes didn't concern me much either.

I acknowledged that their shoes would likely need to be replaced with bigger sizes at some point during the year, and decided we would allow a one-for-one exchange. Too-small tennis shoes could be donated and exchanged for a new pair of larger tennis shoes. Too-small cowboy boots could be given away and replaced with the right size, so my Texas kids could continue to stomp around the neighborhood.

My own wardrobe was sufficient. In fact, clothing was one area I already had experimented with minimalism. A couple years earlier, I stumbled across the idea of capsule wardrobes and it immediately interested me (more on this later). I had been using a limited, forty-item capsule wardrobe, so not buying new clothing for myself wasn't going to be too difficult. My husband, Dave, also got right on board, and recognized that he too had plenty of clothes and shoes to make it through the year comfortably.

As far as holidays and gifts, we decided we would not buy material gifts this year, and rather stick with gifts of experience or consumable items. I was excited to get creative about making our holidays as special as ever, with a new, more intentional perspective. The whole energy surrounding The Challenge was exciting, and creative. I love immersing myself in a new project, and taking on this curious experiment felt like a real adventure. I felt alive and open to progress in ways that you only can when you take a wide step beyond what is comfortable and push yourself to do things differently than you ever have before.

There were surprises along the way, like when we moved

from Texas to Virginia we had to modify our plans to include some fall/winter clothing for the kids. But for the most part, we completed our challenge with flying colors. I can count the exceptions we made on one hand, and throughout the entirety of our challenge I was more dedicated to staying true to the *principles* of The Challenge than the perfection.

The guidelines of The Challenge were not intended to be stifling. Instead, they were created to support us in living more in line with our values. I had always known in my head and heart that relationships and experiences were more important than stuff, but this was an opportunity to apply that value in a meaningful way by making the clear choice to eliminate one and focus on the other.

"When it is
happiness
for sale,
we take one
in each color.

Chapter 2

A BRIEF HISTORY OF CONSUMERISM

Life existed before Target! I know, it's hard for me to believe as well. People have not always been able to find dish detergent on aisle fifteen, tube socks on aisle seven, car batteries on aisle thirty-three, tufted loveseats on aisle seventy, and a smattering of extremely cute and mostly useless knickknacks in the Dollar Spot.

Shopping used to be a function of necessity (and it is important to note that, for most people throughout the world, it still is). Before the age of modern manufacturing, regular people did not entertain the idea of owning more than what they needed for their peaceful, contented lives. It was a time where creativity and enterprise left no place for consumption or acquisition. It was also an age where people found happiness in the small things of life and not in the continuous striving for status and worthiness that modern consumerism sells.

Back then, when you did need something new, there was a very clear path to purchase. You went to the store that carried that particular item. The main street in any town in the developed world was lined with shops selling their handmade wares. Each was specialized and focused on their craft.

The cobbler made, sold, and repaired shoes. The tailor turned cloth into clothing. You would find medicines at a pharmacy where the pharmacist himself was mixing the elixirs behind the counter.

Variety was low, but quality was impeccable. Manufacturing was slow, and it followed that consumption was also slow. The supply of available goods matched the demand. Real people created the products that ended up in your closets and cupboards.

Enter the industrial revolution, which among other things, made mass production of goods the norm. Factories and systems that had been built originally to quickly produce weapons for war shifted supply lines in times of peace to create goods for the people at home. But the speed of manufacturing far outran the speed of regular consumption. A new question emerged in the meetings of manufacturers: How do we entice people to buy things they don't need?

Initially, advertisements were utilitarian, sharing the basic information about the items for sale. They were simple notifications of what was available and how much it cost. But advertisements quickly changed as the agenda emerged within corporations to sell more products than people actually needed.

Rather than sharing information about the product, advertisers aimed to appeal to the emotions of the consumer and make them feel that they needed more to feel happier. These new advertisements promoted and carefully directed people towards the desirable lifestyle, success, and how buying things could improve the relationships of the customer. Obviously it worked!

People buying feelings instead of stuff isn't by accident. The landscape of modern advertising is vast and wide. We are inundated with so many product messages showing us how our lives might look if we just bought this or that. How our lives would feel if we added a little bit more. When it is happiness for sale, we take one in each color.

Social media marketing has moved the needle even further. When you scroll through Facebook, Instagram, or Twitter, the advertisements blend seamlessly into the flow of the feed. They are not only coming from the big companies anymore, they are coming from your favorite bloggers and influencers.

When I started writing a blog as a simple hobby back in 2007 for the purpose of sharing newlywed life with family and friends, I did not realize that eventually the blog would grow an audience, and transform into my business. I had no idea that revenue would eventually come from partnering with companies to promote products I love. (To be honest, I had no idea my little hobby blog would turn into a business at all!)

Because of my awareness of consumer culture, I am very picky about which companies I work with and what products or services I promote. While I still work with companies on sponsored projects on occasion, I turn down far more opportunities than I take, and I aim for transparency with my audience about the behind-the-scenes of what my work looks like.

One of the goals I have with every sponsored post I create is for there to be value delivered to the audience beyond the product, such as a great recipe, an idea for date night, or tips for a more organized pantry space. But even with those clear goals, I can see I have done my job well for the brand when the photo I share of our family picnic is selling quality family time, instead of the new lemonade and ginger ale soda. It is not about the product anymore. It's about the tangible values that the product creates for the consumer and how it makes them value their own life in return.

It is worth mentioning that there are things that people need. Of course some of the products that exist make life easier, more beautiful, and more convenient. Most modern advertising does not give us a chance to really get to know the product itself, because the lifestyle or emotion is what is really being sold.

I had to laugh one day as I was walking past a high-end outdoor goods store. The giant photograph in the window featured an adorable golden retriever dog, slightly wet, sitting in a vintage-style wooden canoe on a misty lake in the mountains. There was not a single product available for purchase featured in the largest advertisement of the store. That, my friends, is emotional advertising. It creates an emotion that makes you want to purchase almost anything!

I knew that The Challenge would affect my business opportunities. It wasn't going to be easy to sell products in a year of not buying products, but I decided it was worth the sacrifice of ad campaigns to live a life more aligned with my values. I was excited to be a quiet voice of reason reminding people they had enough in a world shouting of needs and more and better.

During The Challenge, I only worked with companies to promote consumable goods products. Things that I was actually buying and using in our life during the year. I partnered with great food companies and shared how to create amazing family experiences by cooking together or taking an afternoon to go on a hike and pack a picnic. Choosing to focus on practical minimalism in my personal life allowed me to also focus my blog content on practical tips and conscious advertising. I felt aligned and authentic with my messages.

With the speed of mass production, combined with consistent delivery of emotional advertising, it is no wonder everyone buys stuff all the time. In fact, for a lot of people, the idea that they could simply NOT buy things seems ludicrous.

The day after we began The Challenge, I mentioned to my older sister that we were going to stop shopping for a year. She laughed and responded that she would probably not even make it a week!

Her reaction was not unusual as we began to swim upstream in a rushing current of mindless consumer culture. The question that gives me pause as I reflect over the history of modern consumerism is this: Who gets to choose what I need in my life? Is it me, or the one selling goods disguised as success, joy, and peace?

Am I in the driver's seat of my own shopping, or am I simply reacting to hours and years and decades of finely crafted messaging designed to entice me to buy things I really don't need?

"

At its core, this
new minimalism is
recognizing what
matters most to you
and your family, and
then consciously
disregarding
the rest.

Chapter 3

REDEFINING MINIMALISM

The term "Minimalism" became popular in the early 1960s. A new wave of post-war modern artists were stripping paintings of impressionistic details, portraying wealth and beauty and capturing feelings instead of a true depiction of the world.

What remained was reduced, sleek, and geometric. A parallel movement then happened in music and architecture where the work product was reduced to essential elements. Minimalism was born.

The mantra "Less is More" was not only a description of

the new art and design, but also a wholistic standard to work toward and achieve. A minimalist architect would aim to convey a message of simplicity not only through the physical features of the building but also through the way that the light and materials interacted with the structure.

On a more global level, the term minimalism has also been used to represent a lifestyle stripped down to the bare essentials. In our minds, a minimalist lifestyle often summons images of cold, white rooms, adorned with sleek, lonely chairs, where a very stoic person lives out their life of less. To most of us, the idea of minimalism doesn't sound very cozy, or very fun. We prefer pleasant to stark in our homes and our lives. The idea of "less is more" appeals to us somewhat, but not if it means giving up Black Friday Shopping, or any of our shoes!

But through The Challenge, I was able to implement a more practical type of minimalism in my life that has been over-whelmingly positive. I redefined it in a way that would work for my family as a busy mom of three who loves cake plates and wants to collect all the small brass armadillo figurines. I do not have to adopt an extreme version of minimalism. I do not need to get rid of all of my books and reduce my furniture to one seat per bottom in order to consider myself a minimalist. Instead, I can keep my extra books and chairs while focusing on the main principles of minimalism and applying them in a way that enhances my life.

At its core, this new minimalism is recognizing what matters most to you and your family, and then consciously disregarding the rest. So minimalism as a lifestyle should not have a measuring stick or consistent set of rules. You should not feel that, if you can't be all in and sell your house to live in a studio apartment with a single pair of pants, this lifestyle of less isn't for you. You decide your essential elements. And those essential elements should include any and all things that you love and that bring value to your life. What defines this type of practical minimalism is not how many things you can eliminate but how intentional you are about the things you eliminate and the things you keep around. It's also about being the one who is deciding what you need and not letting advertisement or social media decide for you. It's an empowering place that makes you feel grounded and truthful to your own values.

This more approachable and realistic minimal lifestyle could be called "practical minimalism," "intentionalism," or "conscious consumerism." The guiding principles are: acknowledgment of your abundance, reflection on and evaluation of what things matter most to you and your family, and choosing to intentionally eliminate those things that don't actually matter much to you.

There are sure to be things you own or ways you spend your time that do not add joy to your life. Eliminating those things will free up the space and energy you need to use towards other things you DO value, which will, of course, lead to more happiness and a life of true fulfillment.

How do you discover which things matter most? Begin by considering the last time you felt deeply, abundantly happy and satisfied with the moment. What were you doing? Who were you with? What elements contributed to the joy of that moment?

Chances are, in exploring the moments you have felt deeply, soul-burstingly happy, you will get in touch with your inner values and recognize the things that contribute to this beautiful emotion. These things should absolutely find place in your life and home.

The challenge with deciding on and prioritizing the list of things that we value most is that everyone's list is different. Sometimes, in exploring what we love, we find ourselves alone and it may feel easier to continue to choose what it seems like everyone else is choosing, just so we do not rock the boat. We all love to belong and feel part of a group, from family and friends, to neighbors and communities. One way we relate to each other is by living lives that appear similar. But thinking about your own wishes and values is an essential part of the journey to create the life you want to live, not someone else's life.

There are no rules in practical minimalism. There are no rights and wrongs. The purpose is to eliminate things that are unnecessary (or even detrimental) and promote things that are vital and uplifting. It's about choosing the essential.

PART TWO

PRACTICAL MINIMALISM

"

Knowing ourselves
and trusting what
we love is a critical
element in deciding
when we have enough.

Chapter 4

MORE VS. ENOUGH

That afternoon I looked around the room, suddenly hyperaware of every detail.

The vintage leather Chesterfield sofa sitting in the living room had been on my wish list for years. I had been hunting one down ever since a design blogger had mentioned them in a post on timeless furniture every home needs. I had a home. I guess I needed one.

Eventually the couch manifested itself on Craigslist, and I still cited it as the find of a lifetime. We borrowed our neighbor's truck and picked up the couch within an hour of the listing being posted. In our home over the last few years, it had become even more tattered as my kids and new puppy played on and around its cushions. Right now, I could see those new scratches on our worn, cozy leather couch adding personality and charm to the room.

Above the mantel was displayed an earthy acrylic of the ruins at Mesa Verde. My grandfather painted it back in the 1970s during a weekend art class offered by his long-time employer Geneva Steel. He gave it to me after my grandmother died, mentioning that the grandkids had all wanted her paintings, but wondered aloud why his hadn't yet been claimed. It was one of the few he ever painted and, among all of the other paintings I had collected over the years, this was one of my very favorites.

I looked down. The shoes on my feet were hand-me-down Converse sneakers. Frayed laces and scuffed toes told the stories of hours running around playgrounds with my kids, miles walked discovering Austin, TX right after we moved, and the impromptu dance parties that happened weekly in my kitchen. A friend had given them to me—along with a giant trash bag full of clothes—when she moved away. Downsizing her closet while filling up mine. I wore them almost every day and they felt like second skin.

In our open kitchen shelves I could see a stack of my favorite dishes, like a rainbow of ceramic. Before I bought these plates, we had been using the same set of dishes from our wedding ten years earlier. The sturdy white wedding dishes served us well, and still were in heavy rotation.

But this colorful set was extra special. I collected the watercolor design plates for months—one by one. Every time a plate went on sale at Anthropologie, I added it to the intentionally mismatched set. That way, the table always felt eclectic and (as long as no one fought for the tiger plate) the beautiful designs prompted interesting conversations.

I was reacquainted with all these details and memories because, just moments before, Dave and I had agreed to undergo a year of not buying things. Immediately a switch had flipped in my head. As we committed to not acquiring more stuff, my brain's reaction was to begin taking inventory of our current belongings.

I noticed the wild abundance that filled our kitchen, living room, closets, and every single other area of our life. With the choice to not add more, my survival brain began listing for me everything I already owned that would serve us well during the months of abstaining. I easily recognized in that moment, that what I already had was enough.

Could it really be so simple? Years of consuming, acquiring, and collecting things could be shifted so readily into contentment? All I had to do in order to feel like I had enough stuff was to decide that I didn't need any more? Well, maybe it would get hard later. As I learned to turn off the constant messaging that listed and shouted about all that I needed to be happy. But here, in this very moment, the difference between needing more and having enough had nothing to do with my material belongings at all. It was simply all in my head. Enough wasn't an amount. It was a decision.

. . . . .

This discovery invites the question, if we already have enough, why do we still want to acquire more? The answers are varied and extensive, but most revolve around wanting to feel something different. Whether status, security, happiness, or the idea of success. But maybe it's also about filling our empty spaces with stuff so emptiness doesn't stare right back at us.

Shopping can make us excited. It gives us a little high (but we eventually come down).

We bring something new home, arrange it just-so … and we may never notice it again. The newness wears off as soon as we put it down in our home; it becomes part of what we already have. Off we trot in hot pursuit of something more.

Our brains simply cannot process and bring to mind every detail of our surroundings all the time, so they learn to turn off attention to things that are already there.

With the ever present availability of information in our fast-paced world, we are inundated by the possibility of new things every day. In addition to all of the original methods of advertising with commercials and print ads, now we see them every time we scroll through our Facebook, YouTube, or Instagram feed with current combined active monthly users of over four billion worldwide. That's a lot of people seeing a lot of advertising all the time.

Beyond the paid advertisement, we also see much more of other people's personal lives through social media. Social media is a new advertising tool that introduces us not only to paid media, but also to real people's everyday lives. All of a sudden, everyone is selling something, simply owning and sharing it online. That personal endorsement feels so emotional, that it convinces us even more covertly of the things we should buy. Sometimes the feeling comes from friends and family, and sometimes from the hundreds of strangers who begin to feel like friends. When we get a peek into their homes and lives, we again see new, different, wonderful things that we do not currently own, and we wonder if we should add them to our lives as well.

Months before we began The Challenge, I was walking into H&M to find some new pants for my boys. As I skipped up the stairs to the children's section, I saw a message painted on the wall that declared, "We have new things coming in every day, you should too!"

I realized it was not meant to be literal; however, I was struck by the idea that we as consumers are often following the whims of the retailers, telling us what we need, rather than deciding that for ourselves.

Everywhere we go there are things for sale, all potentially wonderful and new. All offering the hope of happiness, enjoyment, and, in some cases, even prestige or status. It is no wonder that we often have a running list of what more we want to add to our closets, homes, and lives.

In fact, I remember creating an actual, written "to-buy" list in the notes app on my phone several years ago. I guess I wanted to make sure that when some extra money came around for a birthday or something, I was prepared with what I wanted to buy. A couple of the things I remember including were: Ray-Ban Wayfarer sunglasses (I've since realized I do better with inexpensive frames for how often they are lost or broken), and a floral painted water dispenser (I saw one at a boutique and did indeed buy one a couple years later; I've used it a countable number of times, but still think it's beautiful).

. . . . .

That feeling of wanting more when we are out shopping, or at home browsing, reminds me of an early childhood memory. I was ten years old and back-to-school shopping with my dad, a very successful and very thrifty businessman who taught us about money by giving us a budget and then allowing us to choose things for ourselves. In this instance, I had almost spent all of the money allotted for my back-to-school clothes and we wandered into one last store.

In the back of the store, I spotted a denim jacket. It fit perfectly, and was so cool (this was in the early 90s when denim jackets had a heyday). I turned around in it, admiring myself in the mirror.

Yes, I had to have it. This would be my final purchase. I peeled it off and searched for the price tag, and then my face fell.

It was thirty dollars, and I only had fifteen dollars left in my budget. I hoped for an exception, and walked over to find Dad with my siblings on the other side of the store.

I explained and begged and pleaded and tried to negotiate the best I could. "It is the only thing I will ever need again! It is perfect! I will never find another denim jacket as perfect as this!" My dad smiled, and said something I have never forgotten.

"Miranda, there will always be something that you want."

Calmly, he explained that the next time I came back to this store, the denim jacket may not be there, but surely there would be some other wonderful thing in its place for me to be excited about. It was not, in fact, the only perfect piece of clothing in the world, and I would be just fine without it. He said this with such ease and honesty, I knew he was right.

I sulked as I hung that jacket back on the rack, found another something worthy of my last fifteen dollars, and went back home.

If my dad had relented, I'm sure I would have forgotten all about the experience, and that perfect denim jacket. Instead, for over twenty years I think of that lesson every single time I have found myself feeling like I really wanted something that I either don't need or can't afford, or that poses some other difficulty.

Rather than to immediately behave like that child, believing that whatever I saw and wanted, I should own, I began learning that day that some things needed to wait. Our current society doesn't do a great job of preparing children to think before they buy the way my dad did. Instead, those children grow into adults who still believe that just because they like something, that means they should own it. That simply isn't true. It's not always the right time, or the right thing.

"There will always be something that you want."

There is inherent abundance and scarcity in that lesson. "There will always be something ..." tells me the creation of new, exciting, beautiful, and lovely items available to me is ongoing. The world will not run out of denim jackets.

The scarcity comes with the final part: "... that you want."

Our constant desire for more implies a constant lack. If we are not conscious in recognizing our abundance and feeling grateful for what we have and who we are, we will succumb to the underlying idea that we need more. We are wired to seek and find, or click and buy, unless we decide not to.

As much as that moment was a wonderful lesson on budgeting, it has served me better as a reminder of the simple truth that life goes on beyond the things we buy. We don't miss out on all the good stuff by taking a break from shopping, or deciding to say "no" even if we really like something.

We have to take back control of our own accumulation. If we do not, we will continue to bury ourselves in our own houses.

. . . . .

What and how much "enough" looks like varies dramatically and is very individual. I have spent time in parts of the world where smart, happy, wonderful people live in abundance with a one-room home, clothing fitting into a single drawer, and a well for clean water just a mile down the road. My first experience with how little is needed for happiness came when I was still a young girl, just twelve or thirteen years old.

Our family spent Christmas in a small village outside of Guanajuato, Mexico with a humanitarian organization. For a week we slept in tents, practiced our broken Spanish with the beautiful people in the town, and spent the afternoons building water collection systems onto the small, adobe homes from long PVC pipe and giant plastic barrels. My dad, being a contractor, helped manage the teams of volunteers, directing us to haul pipe this way, or hand tools that way.

My mom, a nurse and one of the most naturally friendly people I know, made quick friends with the villagers, encouraging me to sit and talk with them the best I could. To learn about their lives, while at the same time learning a lot about my own. I made friendship bracelets with groups of young children, who were initially shy, and all at once warmed up when they saw I was offering colorful string and stickers.

The sun beat down on the dust-filled town. Cold soda in recycled glass bottles that we bought through the window of a local home, doubling as a kiosk, was an indulgence. Chickens ran wild between the mud houses, sometimes wandering inside one where a single mattress lay pushed into the corner, leaving just enough room for the handmade Lorena stove, a small side table piled with fresh Nopal paddles harvested from the desert outside, and a chair where the matron of the house stationed herself to cook after the day's washing had been scrubbed and hung outside on the line.

I saw joy in the faces of those people. I saw satisfaction after a long, hard day's work. The mothers and fathers loved their children. The children sang songs, played games, and kicked soccer balls as well as anyone I knew. They seemed oblivious to a world I knew: where lights flicked on with the touch of a switch, water ran clear, hot or cold, from any faucet in the house, and food was available in countless varieties from countless vendors.

Let alone the millions of random, mass-produced, household and lifestyle accoutrements that we recognized as not only nice, but necessary. I began to realize that the life I knew was a tiny blip of reality in a world where nothing was a given. The things we needed in our everyday lives were so readily available to us that they weren't valued. Nobody was grateful for having the simple things in life, everyone was on a run for things that didn't even matter that much.

. . . . .

When we get right to it, the essentials of "enough" form basic necessities of shelter, food, clothing, connection, and safety for our families. Anything else is truly more than we need.

That certainly does not mean I advocate for abandoning it all and living on beans. But I find it helpful and humbling to recognize that so much of what we consider to be "not enough" is actually much, much, much more than many people could ever even dream of. That is a good place to begin thinking about what might be enough for ourselves and our families.

I like to consider what I, personally, love and what adds value to my individual life. Knowing ourselves and trusting what we love is a critical element in deciding when we have enough. And so is recognizing things that we don't love and that don't add value to our lives. Being able to easily recognize what things are automatically not valuable for us may make establishing our "enough" even easier.

I love being outside, going on picnics, cooking, reading, camping, design and sewing, decorating, gardening, and playing games with my kids. I love open spaces with lots of light, and fresh greenery. I am most comfortable in casual, neutral clothes that wear well in a variety of situations. I love to travel and experience new things. Recognizing and honoring my own tastes and desires begins to inform me about how much enough might be for me.

I do not love thinking about unnecessary decisions or dealing with any amount of clutter. I do not care much for accessories, and I am not interested in having the latest technology. I do not like high heels, anything with ruffles, or many bright colors. These ideas help me automatically discount things that don't add value to my everyday life. I can appreciate them for other people without wanting to own them myself.

Reflecting on our individual lives and what brings us joy can help give us an idea of what we might actually need, independent of what we see on social media and what works for other people.

As the months passed by during The Challenge, my ability to see what we already had as enough grew even stronger. Through eliminating the possibility of everything I saw being a potential new purchase, I felt more relaxed, content, and peaceful.

I was able to enjoy seeing my friends add things they loved to their lives without automatically wanting more for mine. I loved coming home and really seeing my belongings as just right for now. I didn't feel a lack for anything, and in fact found excitement in going through and donating more and more of what we had that I could see we didn't love, use, or want to care for anymore.

I reclaimed time and energy that otherwise would have been spent browsing online or wandering in stores, and instead used it to do more reading, spending time with the kids, and working on projects that bring me happiness.

Years ago, I was listening to a talk by Michael John U. Teh. One line he spoke shot straight to my heart, and I have been leaning on it ever since:

> "There is no end to what the world has to offer, so it is critical that we learn to recognize when we have enough."

ABUNDANCE EXERCISE

As you read through the last chapter, hopefully you were able to recognize some of the things you already have in your life that bring you joy. You also might have noticed that some of the longings you have for more are actually myths. Perhaps you can see how you might have everything you need today to feel content.

Take a moment and fill out the following myths as they relate to you. These are things that you may have felt even moments ago, that might be false stories now.

MYTH: I will feel happier when I have _____

_____

MYTH: I will feel more successful when I have achieved _____

_____

MYTH: My life will feel more fulfilling once I have _____

_____

Now, take another moment to recognize that all of those feelings of happiness, success, and fulfillment are available to you right now, because they are emotions that are generated by your head and heart. Shift your focus to realize the things available to you in your life right now that can bring those feelings, and fill out the following chart:

TRUTH: I am happy today because of _____

_____

TRUTH: I have achieved success already due to _____

_____

TRUTH: My life is fulfilling right now because of _____

_____

As you shift your thinking to recognize what you have NOW that brings all of the joy and contentment that you need into your life, you will strengthen your ability to recognize enough as a decision not an amount.

When you begin to notice thoughts of needing something more than you currently have in order to feel a certain way, remember that you have access to all of the feelings anytime, because they exist inside of you, and shift your focus back to generating those emotions that you desire within the context of your current circumstance.

"
Through months and
months, each time we
said "no" to more stuff,
it caused a flicker of
gratitude for what
we already owned.

Chapter 5

CULTIVATING GRATITUDE

I cautiously entered the vast warehouse and took a deep breath. This was the first time I had set foot in a Costco since beginning The Challenge two months earlier, and within a few steps I could tell we were in for an adventure. The summer products were already out lining the wide entryway just inside the store.

Giant cardboard boxes were filled with fluffy striped beach towels, colorful plastic insulated coolers, oversized Sunbrellas that converted into shade tents for those upcoming lazy days by the sea, and a whole new line of Tommy Bahama collapsible chairs for soccer games, sporting events, and outdoor picnics.

I leaned in to take a closer look but then snapped myself back into formation. Why was I so easily wooed by the promise of summer adventures and activities? We were here for groceries. We were not buying that stuff.

On the way to the store, I prepared myself mentally with a little pep talk in the car about abundance and gratitude, then I vowed to stick to the shopping list: grapes, apples, almond milk, tortilla chips, soft dinner rolls, Cheddar cheese, and wild caught salmon, among other basic food staples for our meal plan. Everything we needed was in the very back of the store, which meant, of course, that we would have to pass by most of the jam-packed aisles on our way.

I usually do my grocery shopping by myself, while my kids are at school. But on this day the grocery situation at home had gotten a little dire. So even though they were off of school, I piled them in the car and figured we could make it work.

Unsurprisingly, we entered the store and the kids immediately started chirping up—excited about everything that they saw.

"Mom, look at these," my son exclaimed, pointing to the new generation of iPads all lined up like gleaming technological soldiers. "These look so cool, can we get one?"

"They do look cool," I replied. "Isn't it awesome that we have an iPad at home that you get to use sometimes?"

"Wow! Mom! A bounce house! I want one!" My other son was looking up and gesturing at the giant inflatable castle stacked on top of the outdoor equipment and secured to the warehouse ceiling. It really was impressive.

"Yes, buddy!" I exclaimed. "That is amazing! It looks fun to bounce on, just like the trampoline we have in our backyard! Aren't you so glad we have a fun toy like that at home already?"

This continued as we wandered through the store, my kids shouting out about all of the cool, new, exciting things that they saw that they wanted. But rather than just saying "no" and leaving everyone to feel frustrated, I invited the kids to explore the warehouse through the lens of loving what we already had.

It began as an automatic survival method for motherhood: finessing a hard "no" into a subtle "no" that might manage expectations and prevent breakdowns. Soon, the exercise turned it into a game where each time one of my children mentioned an item that they thought was really neat, I challenged them to think of something we had at home that made them feel that same excitement. We would practice feeling gratitude.

The experience reminded me of a favorite old game from the classic movie *Pollyanna*. Our Costco Warehouse version of The Glad Game. Pollyanna was a character in the best-selling novel from the early 1900s, but I knew her from the Disney movie where she was able to put a positive spin on any negative circumstance simply by reframing it. Similarly, as we wandered through the store that day, rather than trying to turn negative situations positive, we used the opportunity to reframe our desire to buy new stuff into gratitude for what we already had.

As we rolled our cart to the back of the store, I thought how incredible it is to not really need any of this beautiful stuff. The box filled with Hawaiian print beach chairs reminded me of similar chairs that I had picked up a few years ago. Ours were no longer clean and bright. In fact, they had frayed edges and stretched-out straps that told stories of the many times that we had hauled them to the beach or on camping adventures.

The result: I found myself feeling quite grateful rather than feeling annoyed that I wasn't buying more stuff. I didn't feel caged in by our decision to stop shopping for the year. Instead, I realized how freeing it was to know exactly what I had come for and not be distracted around every turn.

At the checkout counter, we emptied the cart onto the conveyor belt: grapes, apples, almond milk, tortilla chips, soft dinner rolls, Cheddar cheese, and wild caught salmon, among other basic food staples from my list.

I checked each of the boxes without adding a single extra,

impulsive thing. This may have been the first time in my entire life that I had walked out of Costco without buying a package of socks. Doesn't it seem like everyone always needs socks?

I felt accomplished and excited. A big rush of empowerment as I stuck to my list, stuck to my goals, and left all of those beautiful, fluffy towels in the box for next year. If one little grocery shopping trip could leave me feeling so intentional and grateful for my abundance, what would a whole year do? This experiment was not always going to be easy, but it was definitely worth it.

. . . . .

Gratitude is such a transformative and important practice. I want my kids to grow up seeing their lives through the lens of what is right and good, rather than discontentedly wondering what could be different.

Opportunities to tell my kids "be grateful" arise often in our daily life. I serve potatoes instead of rolls at dinner and when they complain I offer the advice, "When someone serves you food, the only correct response is, thank you!"

After being pestered, one child shares the smaller half of a cookie with another and crying ensues. "That small piece of cookie is better than no cookie!" I say.

A neighbor shows up with a new bicycle and my oldest wonders if he can get a new one, too. "No, honey. You have a great bicycle that you love to ride! Just be grateful for that!"

Over and over I try to teach this idea that what they already have is worthy of appreciation and celebration. At the same time, I find myself oohing and aahing over the pretty new Madewell sandals that just showed up in my inbox (and ARE ON SALE!) and I wonder if I could get some new ones, too!

How often do I stop to tell myself, "No, be grateful for the sandals you already have!" Not because I can't afford them, but simply because I already have some that work. And maybe not buying more sandals helps me love the sandals I already have a little bit better? Maybe exercising some restraint and patience is, in itself, a gratitude practice?

Have you heard the phrase "gratitude practice" before? It is exactly what it describes: an action or set of actions that practices the art and principle of gratitude. Gratitude is often described as an emotion and is possibly even better described as a skill, an action, a coping response, or an attitude. Like any other type of skill, gratitude can be developed and practiced through intentional activities.

One type of gratitude practice, which I had started before The Challenge, is to keep a gratitude journal. From time to time, I write down three things I am grateful for at that moment. My gratitude journaling is sometimes sporadic, but I try to do it daily, or at least a few times a week. And when I am consistent with thinking about, remembering, and actually writing something down, I find that my mind is focused on what is going right throughout the day. As you might expect, I notice more of the good when I am trying to find it.

Another type of gratitude practice, which I have exercised throughout my life, is to write thank you cards when I received a gift or a favor. This practice encourages a moment of pause and reflection. You have to actually be thinking about the gift or favor and whom to thank. Even if just for a brief moment, actively thinking of someone else with an attitude of appreciation builds our own gratitude muscles.

When people experience unexpected loss, whether of family or jobs or opportunities, they often feel a deep sense of gratitude for what remains. Everything feels more meaningful and they wonder how they overlooked it all before. During The Challenge, we were able to hit on some of that gratitude without the pain of loss. Just the absence of more.

Knowing there would not be new clothes, furniture, tech, or toys during the year made us feel that everything we already had was that much more valuable and special. We were able to appreciate each item that brought us joy. We were also able to readily let go of the things that didn't.

In the beginning of that year, I looked to the months ahead with the mindset of a shipwrecked passenger, crawling up on an island and taking inventory of everything that remained from the vessel. These things that already surrounded me would provide comfort, enjoyment, and would be my tools for making it through. A few months in, we had settled into a routine, but still were not taking our belongings for granted.

There was a dusty pink, mid-century style armchair that I particularly loved. I bought it a few months before our minimalist experiment began. But I hadn't given it much thought since adding it to my daughter's room, even though we read stories in it every night.

However, when I walked in to wake her up the morning after The Challenge began, I saw that beautiful chair like it was the first time, and I was filled with gratitude for it. Such a simple, beautiful, useful item that made me happy. Now that I wasn't looking ahead for the next great furniture find, I felt a renewed sense of gratitude for a chair that I already owned.

It may seem silly to talk about feeling abundant gratitude for a pink chair. Or any other material object, for that matter. When we are asked to name three things we are grateful for, most often our first answers aren't material at all. We are grateful for our family, for our health, for our jobs, and good weather.

But consider this: when we are grateful for something, we feel abundance in our life. And that abundance leads to feelings of contentment, connection, and satisfaction. It follows that as we cultivate gratitude for not only our relationships and our experiences, but also our belongings, our material lives will also feel abundant. Maybe then, we won't find ourselves always wanting more.

If you have a special chair (maybe it's not pink) that you love and feel grateful for, you won't be as enticed by a new chair, because you already feel quite content with the one you have. If you feel real and ongoing gratitude for your current summer dresses, or hiking boots, or trampoline, or blender, maybe this contentment and happiness can help form a buffer against all of the messaging telling us that we should upgrade to the shinier and better ones.

As you focus on practicing gratitude for simple things like your favorite shoes, you are building your gratitude muscle so that it may be flexed to feel grateful for more important things like your health or a sense of community. Operating within that gratitude creates confidence, contentment, abundance, and lasting joy. This inner happiness makes you then appreciate the incredible people and relationships in your life.

Do you see them? Are you all filled up by the incredible life that you are living?

Through months and months, each time we said "no" to more stuff, it caused a flicker of gratitude for what we already owned. Or sometimes, saying "no" to something I didn't need simply made me feel grateful for my freedom and opportunity to choose.

GRATITUDE PRACTICE

While cultivating gratitude through simply not shopping is effective, there are lots of other ways to practice gratitude in our everyday life. Here is another short practice that you can use on a regular basis.

I invite you to pause for a moment and look around you. What things do you see that are helpful tools for your daily life? Wherever you are, whatever your day has been like, there is a sense of abundance in your life, regardless of your belongings.

- Close your eyes for a moment and think about something good that has happened to you recently. Think about how that felt. Allow yourself to feel it again. From the top of your head to the tips of your toes, feel filled up by that happiness.
- Now think about someone you love. Picture their kindness towards you and how much you care for them. Feel that love inside of you.
- Write these things down on a piece of a paper, or a note in your cell phone. Look over the list or make a new one every couple days in order to cultivate gratitude and content.

Here are Eleven More Ideas for Cultivating Gratitude in your every-day life. They seem simple, but they are effective.

. . . . .

1. SAY THANK YOU MORE OFTEN

Think about the hundreds of times each day that we have the opportunity to say thank you and verbally express gratitude for something that someone has done for us. Being thankful makes you identify what is truly essential.

2. COUNT YOUR BLESSINGS

Take a moment to list out the things that you are grateful for right now in your life. There are so many things that we just take for granted because we're so incredibly blessed.

3. STOP COMPLAINING

As we complain, we train our brain to recognize what is wrong with whatever situation we're facing because we are taking the time to notice it and then say it. We're creating these pathways ourselves. If you start vocalizing the things that are good instead you are actually teaching your brain to recognize the good!

4. PLAY THE GLAD GAME

When you feel a little bit down or negative about something, consider what are the positive spins that you can put on it? Take a moment to actually discover what is the silver lining on whatever problem or situation you are facing.

5. SMILE

The act of smiling actually boosts the hormones in your brain. The happy hormones as you smile tell your body that some-thing good has happened. You're telling your body that you are happy and excited. Even if at first you fake it, putting on a smile works wonders for your mood.

6. SPEAK WELL OF OTHERS.

It's so important to treat people well in person and to speak well of them when they are not with us. When we speak well of others in their presence and in their absence, we are naturally inviting ourselves to consider the good about those people while naturally tuning ourselves to the channel of what is positive.

7. WRITE A THANK YOU CARD.

Training our minds to feel grateful can happen through a physical act like writing a thank you note for something simple. Taking a couple minutes to physically engage in gratitude as you write and send a thank you note will boost your gratitude and overall well-being, as well as connect you more fully to the different recipients as you consider how you appreciate them.

8. USE THE THINGS YOU LOVE.

When we use the things we have, we love them even more. We are able to feel grateful for them as we're using them. This also helps train us to recognize what we really do love and what types of things can benefit our daily life. So grab those nice dishes from the cabinet and use them!

9. WRITE DOWN THE GOOD AND THE THINGS YOU'RE GRATEFUL FOR.

The act of writing down—rather than just thinking about— makes you question and internalize what gratitude means to you. As you begin to write down what you appreciate about each day, you will find yourself noticing more of the good things that happen in your everyday life.

10. HELP OTHERS.

By helping someone else, we can recognize that we have more than enough. This feeling of content then allows you to create more space for others, to share with them and help them. Giving creates gratitude.

11. PRAY AND MEDITATE ON THE THINGS THAT YOU ARE GRATEFUL FOR.

Spend just a quiet moment in prayer or meditation, it becomes an intentional moment of acknowledging that we're connected to so many things greater than ourselves. There's something really special about feeling part of something bigger than your own life.

"Sometimes we
choose to wait,
and sometimes life
chooses for us.

Chapter 6

THE POWER
OF PATIENCE

The sun was shining joyfully, and the happy mood trickled down into our hearts. Texas was known for its sunshine, and in the three years since we had made Austin home, it had not disappointed us. My three kids scampered around the neighborhood playground playing tag with their friends while I sat on the nearby bench and caught up with mine.

"How are the kids doing with The Challenge?" one friend asked. "Mine would have a fit if I told them we weren't buying new toys for a year!"

"Mine have a fit even when we do buy them new toys!" another laughed, and we all nodded knowingly.

"They're actually doing amazing!" I commented. "I've been surprised by how adaptable they are, and how easily they have understood the guidelines we created."

I really was surprised. I had been curious to see what my little ones thought about our decision to not buy things this year. What would that mean to them, at their young ages of seven, five, and three? I was prepared for a lot more battles than we had faced so far. In fact, they almost seemed to not be affected. Maybe my apprehension was all a projection of my own insecurities. They didn't lack for anything. We had a playroom filled with toys they loved, closets stacked with clothes that fit, and a home designed to invite coziness and love.

I turned back to my friends to share a little more. "Do you want to hear one thing they have started doing that makes me smile?" I asked. "When we go into the store for groceries or household supplies, they always ask to visit the toy aisles. They know we aren't going to buy anything, but they tell me they like to see the toys anyway."

I laughed a little bit thinking about this curious habit all of my kids had picked up in the last few months that both made me happy and gave me a new perspective.

"When we walk through the toy section, they each choose one or two things that are their very favorites. Then they turn to me and ask, 'Mom, can I have this next year?'"

It was April 2017. "Next year" meant 2018, when The Challenge was over. Eight months was a long time to wait for a toy!

The other moms' eyes all widened, and they smiled. My kids' requests were cute for sure!

"So, are you keeping a list of all these toys to buy in the new year?" another giggled.

"No," I said. "Every time we go to the store, the toys they love change, and they have forgotten all about the ones they wanted before. It seems more like a game. A ritual of seeing the new exciting things, and feeling the rush of happiness when I tell them that sure they can have it next year. Then they go on happily without actually buying anything!"

"They're learning some patience," another friend interjected. "What a great lesson for them at their ages."

I glanced over to the swings where my oldest was pushing my youngest as she giggled gleefully.

"Yes," I replied. "It has been a good lesson for all of us!"

. . . . .

When Dave and I sat down that first night in January to discuss the goals of The Challenge, developing patience had been high on the list. Choosing to wait to buy something until the year was over would be a direct application of the principle of patience. It was something I looked forward to working on. I would never have called myself a patient person, yet I believed in the value and power of patience as a virtue. I was excited to dig in and learn more.

My personal impatience manifested itself more in recklessness than in anger or frustration. During most of my life, rather than waiting for help or waiting for someone to give me instruction or permission, I would move forward with whatever project or assignment I wanted to work on. I was fiercely independent, sometimes to a fault.

On occasion, that impatience resulted in misunderstanding and needing to redo the work. Other times, it resulted in what looked like and felt like the efficient accomplishment of my projects. I didn't even recognize a lot of my impatience because I labeled it "autonomy," "determination," or "getting stuff done."

Where lack of patience came back to bite me was in situations where I didn't have the control to forge ahead without the help or support of someone else. When a life circumstance was beyond my ability to manipulate or reinterpret, then I felt lost.

. . . . .

Sometimes, waiting is unnecessary and doesn't make a big impact on the result. For example, when Dave and I decided to get married. Over the course of a sixty-minute conversation, what began as a beautiful spring outdoor wedding morphed into a beautiful beginning of October fall affair. It was July. But, "Why wait?" we decided, and three whirlwind months later we became husband and wife.

We both agree that just making it happen was the best decision we ever made. Those extra months between October and May—what would have been waiting—became instead a head start on our new life together. With each of the holidays that passed those first few months we would look at each other and laugh, "Remember how we wanted to wait to get married? It's so great we didn't wait because this is so much fun!"

. . . . .

Other times, though, waiting is the only option. Soon after my oldest son Milo was born, I was already excited about having another baby. He was a lovely, happy infant, and although I was exhausted, I looked forward to growing our family. I was certain Milo would be a fantastic big brother.

Sharing a positive pregnancy test with Dave when Milo was just ten months old seemed crazy, but we were elated. I soaked in the feeling of growing another life. For several weeks I planned and scheduled and prepared for the months of pregnancy.

We were out of town visiting family when I started to bleed. Spotting at first, then more. I was terrified, but hopeful. It would all be okay, right? When we returned home the next day the doctor saw us right away. The ultrasound showed a developing yolk sac, but no viable fetus. No heartbeat. No life.

Later that night I curled into a ball on the cold ceramic surface at the bottom of the bathtub and let the shower fall like rain onto my aching body and aching heart. In an instant my plans were all washed away. The hope for this new baby had filled me up, and I felt like the wind had been knocked out of me. I couldn't breathe.

The next couple months were a crash course in patience. There was no way to forge ahead alone on this journey of growing a family. I was simply not in control. I had to wait. I filled my days with healing, planting an herb garden on the apartment patio, and joining a running group. The time I spent with Milo felt holy. I hugged him tightly and let him linger in my arms before laying him in bed at night.

During my waiting, I also questioned. "What am I supposed to learn from this?" "How do I prepare for not knowing what happens next?" "When will our family get to grow?"

One day I came across a phrase that hit home. It was part of a longer poem, but the piece that jumped into my heart was this, "… nor doubt, nor rush, but hush, for God is here."

The word "rush" especially resonated with me. What was the rush? I was only twenty-seven! Why was I in such a hurry for my whole life to roll forward right now? Wasn't this moment, too, incredible? I had a beautiful baby boy, a husband whom I adored, a great job, lovely apartment, group of friends and neighbors that felt like family. Right now I could be happy. Right now, I had all I needed.

I wrote that phrase onto our entry mirror so that every time I came inside, I saw the reminder to be patient. This wasn't a nagging, angry, resentful type of patience. This patience was peaceful. This patience was active. It felt like vibrant hope and happiness. Trusting that life would be beautiful even if it was beyond my control. This patience was waiting, without doubt or questions. Waiting while simultaneously living really well.

Most of us are familiar with the idea of patience. We think of it as waiting for what we want. How can we go beyond the simple waiting into an understanding of next-level patience where we recognize the long-term power of postponing some immediate gratification for a bigger, more inspiring and more impactful long-term goal? Sometimes we choose to wait, and sometimes life chooses for us. Either way, we can transform the waiting into an experience of learning, growth, development, and inspiration if we focus on the beauty of the present while also maintaining enthusiastic anticipation of the future. We are no longer passively patient but becoming active in that form of patience—it is truly empowering.

Months later, a few days after finishing my first half-marathon with my beaming baby boy and incredible husband cheering me on, I shared another positive pregnancy test with Dave. The journey had begun again, this time without expectation or rush. I had begun to learn about how patience and even resilience not only sounded like a good idea, but actually transformed the way I felt. It invited peace. It allowed joy.

. . . . .

As my kids started growing into toddlers, and then actual children, they learned to communicate what they wanted. They didn't understand why they couldn't have everything right this second. A simple "not right now" from me could turn on a tantrum that affected our whole afternoon. I found myself explaining patience to my four-year-old by saying, "Patience is waiting, happily, without asking questions."

The "without asking questions" stemmed from hundreds of conversations that turned "no" into "why?" and "when?" and "now is it time?" These tiny people echoed the same questions I usually felt when faced with a circumstance that required my patience.

"Why?" "When?" "Now is it time?"

I wanted to teach this important principle in a specific way, even though I was still very much learning how to exercise patience in my own life. After lots of pondering, I came upon the idea that there might be two kinds of patience: a true kind of patience that brought peace and a false kind that invited complaining or frustration. "Waiting, happily, without asking questions" was a patience that felt like being content with whatever today brought. We could allow the circumstance beyond our control to be what it was, while we focused on things that we could appreciate in the moment.

. . . . .

That's not to say that every scenario was happy. While my kids did adapt incredibly well to The Challenge, there were days that the decision to not just buy the dang thing made us all a little grumpy.

My daughter Plum, who was three, lost two pairs of shoes within the first month. We had decided that buying replacement items would be allowed within our guidelines, but the idea was that the replacement would be like the original. Tennis shoes for tennis shoes. Boots for boots.

When I took Little Miss Plum to the shoe store to find a new pair of tennis shoes to replace the pair she had lost somewhere between our house, the neighbor's house, and the pool, she immediately fell in love with every pair of sparkling, shiny, glitter-dusted high heels on the display. "Mama! Wook at dose sparkawee pwincess shoes!" she cried with delight.

I tried to redirect her toward the tennis shoes, but it was hopeless. The girl loves her glitter. I let her play with the sparkling heels while I found a suitable pair of replacement sneakers. But after being twitterpated by sparkles, the simple pink and blue pair in my hand were beyond uninteresting. Plum was not impressed. She wanted the heels. But we were not going to get the heels.

Not only was she three years old and I thought it was ridiculous they even made glittery heels for children so young, we absolutely did not need another pair of "princess shoes." Plum had a pair of gold flats that she hadn't lost (yet), and they were perfect for dressing up for church, or wearing with play clothes. What she no longer had was a pair of tennis shoes that she could wear to school and running around actively outside!

The easiest thing would have been to just buy the shoes she wanted. They weren't that expensive, they would make this child happy, and what was one more pair of tiny shoes? But I remembered The Challenge. I reminded her of the princess shoes she already had and loved. I told her we were going to get these amazing pink princess tennis shoes that would be so fun to play in, and hugged her close to remind her we could come back next year and get those sparkly shoes. Then, as we started back toward the register, she burst into tears.

She cried all the way home. Of course she did. She was three years old and didn't get the pair of sparkly princess heels that she wanted! Crying is what most three-year-olds would do! Maybe I should have let one pair of princess shoes slide. I considered that maybe it hadn't been that big of a deal. But adding that one pair of shoes that we simply didn't need to the dozens of similar, tiny, unnecessary purchases that we make in any normal year and you would get exactly what life had been before we decided to make a change at all.

. . . . .

This whole challenge was about eliminating those small, unnecessary purchases to develop a greater sense of intention, abundance, gratitude, and patience. From the adults right on down to the kids—even my sweet three-year-old. And maybe one small moment didn't seem very important. But if one small moment didn't make a difference, then what would?

Life is nothing but a series of small moments all layered together to create our experience. Now, more than ever, when instant gratification drives the way we eat, shop, and spend our time, paying attention to what happens in the small moments of intentional, active patience drives the change that we need in order to become the people we want to be.

I had always heard that "good things take time," but until we put into practice some of these principles in a way that shaped our small, daily decisions and habits, I don't know that I understood how that worked. Sometimes you cannot see the power of one decision until it is layered with hundreds of other small, similar decisions. Then, you back up, and see how those choices shaped your life. Let's go beyond level one patience, where we simply wait for things when necessary, to next-level patience, where we are actually reaping the long-term benefits of actively appreciating the wait. Let's invest in our future families, lives, and selves by not always choosing the simple, easy "yes" today in favor of a bigger, more powerful "yes" to becoming the people we hope to be, and living the life of our dreams.

· · · · ·

Patience is not developed through waiting, happily, for one day. Patience is developed by waiting, happily, one day at a time for weeks and months and sometimes years. Waiting, happily, while choosing to be resilient and finding happiness where you are regardless.

· · · · ·

What things in your own life require you to exercise patience? Have you given much thought to the value of waiting, happily, within the life circumstances that you cannot control?

As a generation, our ability to wait is rapidly diminishing because we have very little to wait for. You can order anything online and have it on your porch within two days, sometimes two hours. You can book a plane ticket with the click of your thumb, and book an Uber with a different click of the same thumb.

Food is fast, fashion is fast. Friendships and relationships are only a swipe away. Entertainment in every form dances within the rounded-edge, rectangular borders of our screens. So why would you choose to wait for anything?

Maybe because good things take time. Maybe because there will be a circumstance or challenge in your life that you can't click away, and without knowing how to wait, happy, you will feel yourself start to fall apart.

. . . . .

To bring you full circle on the story I shared at the beginning of this chapter, I need to share that when the calendar turned over into the new year, my kids didn't ask for all of the toys that they had been excitedly enjoying in the store for the whole year. They didn't really want them. They didn't really need them at all.

What they did have at the end of the year was an emotional tool kit filled with experiences of times they had waited for something they wanted, and survived. Thrived, even. Those experiences of practicing this next-level, active patience will serve them for the rest of their lives, much more than any toy ever could.

WAITING CHART

During The Challenge, I found that patience, like other values and virtues, requires practice. Here are a few ways you could practice patience in your own life with small circumstances that aren't life-altering.

You will find as you practice patience in the small, seemingly insignificant things, you will have more of it in the moments you really need it. Give some of my examples a try and fill in some of your own, specific to your life and needs.

Wait **ten seconds** and take a deep breath before you:

- ▷ yell at anyone
- ▷ say an unkind word
- ▷ eat a snack
- ▷ honk at another driver
- ▷ _____
- ▷ _____

Wait **one hour** and take a deep breath before you:

- ▷ look at your phone in the morning
- ▷ accept a new role or responsibility
- ▷ begin an argument
- ▷ _____
- ▷ _____

Wait **one day** and take a deep breath before you:

- ▷ buy something you haven't planned on ahead of time
- ▷ make a big decision
- ▷ _____
- ▷ _____

As you bring some awareness and intention into moments that you feel impatient, you will begin to automatically make positive progress toward developing patience. Remember, powerful patience is waiting, happily, without asking questions. Focus on living presently.

"

That focus on all-or-nothing
success is what keeps so
many people from trying,
learning, and living out
their dreams.

Chapter 7

IMPERFECT MINIMALISM

Registration was full and my first hand-painted textile class was starting in an hour. I showed up to the venue, arms full of dish towels, paint brushes, liquid dye, and canvas drop cloth. While I had been teaching craft workshops for several years, today would be my first time teaching this particular craft. It was also my first time teaching at Vintage Fresh, a small, beautifully curated boutique in North Austin. On top of that, the following morning I was hopping on a plane to Salt Lake City for a blogging conference. A blogging conference for which I still had to pack and finalize a presentation. But I set aside my internal hurry so I could focus on what was happening right now: the workshop.

I was hoping to make a good impression on Leslie, the owner of Vintage Fresh. A mutual friend had introduced me to Leslie a few months before. I loved her beautiful shop filled with refinished mid-century furniture, southwestern-inspired home decor, potted cactus and succulents, and a handful of locally made bags and textiles. A perfect fit for my desert-inspired designs, and the laid-back, friendly vibe of my classes.

We set up the table and chairs, pulling everything together with name cards. Then, with the few minutes before class began, I browsed the store, oohing and aahing about the beautiful wares.

This type of boutique—more than any of the big box stores at the mall or online—was where I felt most tempted to buy things. This was a shop where I knew the owner, and could give her a hug. Every purchase made at this local business had a direct impact on her family. Almost everything aligned beautifully with my style. Still, it was all stuff I could go without, stuff I really didn't need.

The workshop was a success. A dozen women learned and laughed together, painting delicate and bold cacti on the white cotton towels. We admired each other's work, and appreciated the variety of color choices and styles. I always feel a buzzy, happy energy when I host and teach workshops, and tonight was no different. Bringing people together to learn and create has always been one of my passions, and I was thrilled with the opportunity.

As the newly painted textiles hung to dry, I reminded the workshop attendees that they each would receive a discount on any purchases they made in the shop before they left. It was a standard piece of the workshop collaboration agreement, and a chance for the shop to benefit even further from hosting my class. Everyone milled around, chatting and shopping. One by one people collected their purchases, hand-painted towels, and goodbye hugs, then left.

Leslie and I finished cleaning up, rinsing paint brushes and rolling the long, canvas tablecloth into a wad for washing. I tucked things into my boxes and walked over to the register to finish details, when I noticed a small, olive-colored laptop bag on the top shelf across from the cash wrap.

It was made by another local company, and was marked to half-price. Normally ninety dollars, the red sticker read forty-five dollars, and as I pulled it from the shelf for a closer look, Leslie mentioned it was also on clear-out, plus with my workshop discount it would be just over twenty dollars.

In a moment of practicality and maybe the smallest hint of rebellion against my own set of no-shopping rules, I bought it. I was leaving in ten hours for a cross-country flight, and would be working on the conference presentation on my laptop while I traveled. I didn't actually own a proper laptop bag. This would be so easy, and so helpful. I also really liked the idea of giving a vote of support and thanks, however small, to Vintage Fresh at the end of a great partnership.

The rules we set out at the beginning of the year dictated that if I needed something, I could choose to make it with materials I already had on hand. I knew that I had a pile of canvas, zippers, and maybe even all of the hardware I might need for a similar bag in my sewing room at home—but what I didn't have a lot of was time. Or energy, to stay up all night making something that I could really use right now.

I did have the remains of an old, handmade laptop sleeve that I had sewn years ago for a different computer—it was something. But, I felt like this one was just right in every way: locally made, locally sold, on sale, and I could see how it would immediately make my life a little easier.

The truth was, I didn't need it. I easily could have left it there and made do with one of the several backpacks or tote bags that I already owned or, like the last time I flew with my laptop, wrapped it in a sweatshirt and stuffed it in my carry-on. It survived the sweatshirt. So I could have done what I had already been doing for five months straight: saying "no," while feeling gratitude for all of the ways I could make do without, and "I'll get it next year," while exercising my patience.

And after all that, I still made the deliberate decision to buy it. The beauty of the decision, though, was that it was deliberate. Not a whim, not a fluke. I had paused to think and consider whether or not this item would add value to my life for the long term, and intentionally decided that it would! That intention was a win, rather than a failure.

Leslie followed along with my life and blog enough to know that we weren't buying things this year. When I told her, "I'm going to take it," she looked a little surprised and laughed that she wouldn't tell anyone. I mentioned that I planned to share about it. Not because the laptop bag itself was very significant, but because one purchase wasn't going to derail me from my larger goals of developing gratitude, abundance, and focusing on all I had.

Buying one simple thing that I hadn't planned on didn't feel like the end to The Challenge, but part of the process of hopping off the horse and still choosing to get back on. I wasn't failing, or giving up. I didn't plan to take the night off and hurry to buy a pile of things that I had been writing on a list somewhere. I was making a decision to break one of my own rules, and then obey them again. Part of the beauty of The Challenge was that it was personal. We had invented it. We had the freedom to choose.

I went home and packed my laptop up properly, tucking the cords into the perfect pockets of the new bag. It made flying the next day super easy to have the computer in an easy-to-access place. I loved having it feel slim and sleek, with just enough room for my business cards, phone and cord. Totally not necessary, but so very useful. And a great introduction to the imperfect, write-your-own-rules minimalism that we would pick up after this year of The Challenge ended. In the meantime, I got back to not buying things.

. . . . .

Perfection is elusive, isn't it? Lucky for me, I was born without much of a perfectionism gene, and have grown up measuring myself by effort, not achievement. Maybe that's why, when I embarked on The Challenge, I was one hundred percent confident we would succeed. Because to me, success didn't look like literally not buying one single extra, unnecessary, non-consumable good for twelve months straight. That was the goal, and I believe goals are there to point us in the right direction. The progress is found in the process.

True, lasting success in The Challenge would mean deepening our gratitude, practicing patience, and choosing to see abundance in our life in a way we hadn't seen it before. The method we chose was not buying extra stuff—and if for some reason I made a decision here or there to buy one thing, that didn't mean The Challenge was over and we went home empty-handed. It meant we were learning, and trying, and moving the needle towards a more intentional, mindful, and minimal lifestyle.

The risk of sharing my feelings about perfection as it relates to The Challenge is that some of you perfectionists will discount the validity of our effort and accomplishment because I admit there were a couple times we bought something that wasn't in line with our original plan. You might be thinking to yourself right now, "How can you talk about a year without shopping when you literally just told us about you shopping?"

Yes, I admit this whole story would have been a lot more tidy with a no-fail, one hundred percent no non-consumable purchased record, and a zero percent adjustment rate, but that wasn't reality. That focus on all-or-nothing success is what keeps so many people from trying and living out their dreams.

Have you ever had a friend (or yourself) on a diet that cheated by eating a cookie, and then ended up eating the whole bag because, why not? The diet was shot anyway! Do you know someone who started a daily exercise program and missed one single day, so they stopped exercising for six months straight? I do. And I believe that giving up the process of progression because of one misstep or exception is a waste of so much potential.

We don't grow in a straight line. We meander and make mistakes. We try, and try again. If perfect is the requirement for success in life, we all fail big time. Being perfect is an unrealistic reality.

What if, rather than seeking perfection, we simply committed to do our best—whatever that looks like—every day? Our best on a sunny day that we wake up feeling healthy and the kids get to school on time and the house is miraculously sort of picked up, might be very different than our best on a day that it is raining and we wake up with a headache and the kids all complain through breakfast and someone slips and falls on the way to carpool and last night's dishes are still all piled up in the sink. What if our best was simply us trying hard to live a good, intentional life day after day?

We would all be much healthier if eating a cookie was just a simple choice and we went right back to eating healthier foods after the last bite. So many of us would be in much better shape if missing one day of exercise meant we start again tomorrow, no shame for the omission, no questions asked.

During The Challenge, we had to make a couple pivots here and there. My first unplanned purchase was that laptop bag, that I can proudly report I have used every day since. It has added so much value and ease to my life and workflow as I travel for speaking, teaching, and even just from home to my studio office.

I don't regret it one bit, both because it's a really great bag and, more than that, because it allowed me the chance to think deeply about the gifts of imperfection. It helped me see that the success or failure of a big, life-changing experiment like the one we undertook as a family was not made or broken by one single purchase, but by the shifting lens through which I was able to measure our efforts.

Even the fact that I had given buying or not buying the bag a second thought was an indication of mindfulness and intention that had definitely not existed before The Challenge began. It was not a mindless purchase.

I was growing and changing as a consumer, and as a person. And even in the middle of a self-imposed challenge, I was able to make choices without shame. We made the rules, and we adapted them as necessary to serve our needs while still remaining true to the principles we set out to develop. This flexibility and grace with myself came in handy as we faced several unexpected experiences during The Challenge that I was able to navigate with confidence.

For example, halfway through the year we moved from Texas to Virginia. As part of our move, we decided to downsize our living area to 1000 square feet and continue experimenting with minimalism. Going from three bedrooms to two, and three bathrooms to one, meant our furniture and belongings just wouldn't line up exactly right. While we had intended to not buy any new furniture this year, we adjusted that guideline to allow for the replacement of two bedrooms' worth of kids' beds and dressers to one new bedroom set that included a triple bunk bed and one small six-drawer dresser.

If we had been committed to perfection instead of principle, we wouldn't have been able to flexibly buy new furniture to replace the many pieces we sold and donated. During our move, I estimate we decreased our overall belongings by over forty percent. That decrease, combined with our commitment to not acquiring more through mindless shopping, meant our life became a lot less cluttered, all at once. By allowing ourselves the flexibility to live true to the spirit of The Challenge, we actually moved the needle even further towards the intentional lifestyle we desired.

If you believe in imperfection as a gift and an opportunity for growth, rather than a weakness or failure, you might be more willing to push yourself beyond what feels comfortable right now. You might be excited to try something new that would elevate and inspire your life. You might have the confidence to move boldly in the direction of your dreams, without worrying so much about the details. If you believed that you could buy less but better, and trusted yourself to choose wisely what that meant for you and your family, I am certain your life would feel more free.

Sometimes when I share about The Challenge, those listening will tell me they could never do it. Never be a minimalist. Never stop shopping. But I think they could. Imperfectly, probably. It doesn't have to be one or the other. Imperfect practical minimalism simply means doing your best to think before you buy.

Choose what matters most. There is something in the concept of perfection that consumerism will always use to convince people that getting this item will make their life truly perfect. It's an illusion. Perhaps imperfect minimalism is also about recognizing that we as human beings are not perfect and never will be. We can try our very best but it's in the imperfection where we find values and strength that allow us to live with intention and awareness. We all can do that.

SHOULD I BUY THIS? FLOW CHART

As you make decisions about what things will truly be great purchases and which to leave in the store, you may find asking yourself a few questions to be a helpful practice. There are a few key questions I like to ask myself when faced with a decision about whether or not to bring something home. As I have used this idea in my own life, it reminded me of a flow chart, one question leading to the next. I asked my friend Becky Simpson, flowchart extraordinaire, and owner/artist behind Chipper Things (chipperthings.com), to create a custom flow chart just for this question!

The next time you are wondering "Should I Buy This?" follow the flow to the end of the chart and you'll have an intentional, thoughtful, and practical answer. You may discover that the answer isn't always "Yes!"

Should I Buy This?

PART THREE

LESS STUFF

"The kids simply
played with what
was there, without
worrying about
what wasn't.

Chapter 8

LESS STUFF = MORE FOCUS

held my breath and waited for a fall-out as the kids ran into the playroom for quiet time. While they were at school I had systematically organized their toys and books, eliminating well over half of the stuffed animals, action figures, trucks, and blocks from the bins beneath the window.

I was careful to only remove those toys that never seemed to be played with. The ones they tossed onto the floor as they dug for what they were really looking for. But I was curious to see if they would notice, or if they would simply play with their favorites without feeling the loss.

Toys had always been a complicated dance for me as a mom.

I loved a few simple toys. My very favorites were the artsy wooden variety that cost way more than expected and looked prettier than they might have actually been fun.

I found a few affordably priced wooden blocks, cars, and rattles at flea markets and a couple special ones at museum art shops and posh baby boutiques. I also had a thing for small, plastic animal figures. We had a whole set of really amazing plastic dinosaurs, and enough other animals to fill a tiny zoo.

These types of toys felt to me like the kind that inspired imagination. They didn't presuppose a certain type of play, instead invited the child to create new worlds and invent new games.

They were also much more exciting for me than my kids, who seemed to flock to anything with lights and stickers, and if it made sounds it was a surefire hit. So I compromised.

I would keep the artsy toys I loved as decoration, if nothing else. They would live on shelves and night stands. The other toys would live in bins or baskets, out of sight when not being actively played with. Only the errant (and disconcerting) "beep" or "boop" coming from the bins in the middle of the night to remind us of their presence.

In the years since we first began collecting toys, I had tried several different systems to keep them stored, organized, and accessible without taking over the whole house. I rarely bought toys myself, yet between birthday parties, Christmas gifts, and grandparent visits, we amassed a healthy pile in a few short years. I found myself cursing the seemingly bottomless bins of toys.

We had baby dolls and race cars, Lego sets and army men, remote control cars and electronic action figures. The playroom was meant to be a place to play, but so often the floor was covered entirely in toys and, because of the mess, the kids would bring their chosen play thing into the kitchen or living room to have space to actually play.

Something had to give. It was our year of letting go of stuff in exchange for gratitude, patience, and abundance. So, while the kids were at school, I had systematically reduced the excess to create room for "enough."

In some ways, the toy purge had been emotional for me. At seven, five, and three, my kids weren't babies anymore, and even though they had developmentally passed beyond needing stacking rings and sensory balls, actually donating them felt like acceptance of a new chapter in my life as a mom.

I comforted myself by conjuring up an image of another young mom hitting the jackpot as she stumbled upon a whole bag of almost-new baby toys at the thrift store. Deep breath. This was good for me ... and for her.

Five minutes into quiet time, I peeked through the doorway of the room and saw the boys happily building with Lego, their current favorite activity. Plum was giggling as she pulled books off of the shelf, which was her favorite activity. No one seemed to notice that the toy bins were lighter and the room a bit emptier—except for me. And I was thrilled!

. . . . .

Deciding to not buy non-consumable goods for a year didn't only impact Dave and me, but our children as well. The morning after our decision to undergo The Challenge, we sat together around the breakfast table and presented our plan. The boys, being a bit older, understood that we were saying no new toys or clothes until next year. They seemed unconcerned about clothes, but curious about the toys. What would happen if they wanted a new toy?

Until that point, although I wasn't buying toys and games weekly, it was not unusual for us to motivate good behavior or household chores with a trip to the toy aisle for an inexpensive addition. I always wondered how worth it that really was, as they seemed to misplace and break their toys as often as we bought new ones.

I explained that if we needed something new to play with, we could be creative! We could use craft supplies to make something, or go outside and find some sticks and rocks to use as toys (a game they played all the time, anyway). We talked about how we could make a list of special toys they wanted and consider buying them after the year was over. If they happened to get a toy in a happy meal or at a birthday party, we wouldn't take them away. We just wouldn't buy them any ourselves.

As the year went on, I slowly and intentionally pared down our toy collection. Every time I removed a few things, I wondered how it would affect the kids' play time. Not at all, it turned out!

The kids simply played with what was there, without worrying about what wasn't. Not only that, but they seemed to play happier and longer with fewer toys to decide between. They no longer had to make big decisions or big messes before getting into an imaginary scenario with their tiny Lego men or baby dolls.

I shouldn't have been surprised. I knew full well that kids adapt easily to playing with less. On vacation, they make up games with travel-size soap containers. On the beach they play for hours with seaweed and sticks. They never complain about not bringing all their toys on family camping trips. Why would it be any different at home?

My first experience with toys as a mom had been years before, in a small apartment in the Washington DC area. We had moved there for Dave's graduate studies when Milo was just four months old, and settled into a 900 square foot apartment easily. Since there wasn't a proper playroom, I stored the bins of fresh-smelling baby toys in baskets in the living room where they could both be easily accessed and easily hidden.

During the day, I would lay out a blanket, put little Milo down on the floor, and surround him with brightly colored toys to grab and toss. We rolled balls together, built block towers, and shook that little geometric wood and elastic bell rattle until our ears rang. The toys were easy to toss back into the basket at the end of play time, and after bedtime the living room felt like a relaxing place to hang out with friends and enjoy some cozy conversation.

A couple years and another baby later, the apartment was feeling a little smaller, and two small toy baskets no longer accommodated our collection. Rather than give any away, I started to rotate them. One box of toys went into our small storage closet in the basement while a few lived in the living room bins. Every few months I would switch the toys out, and it was as if the kids had a whole new set, even though they weren't truly new.

It seemed like a good system. My boys were happy, and the apartment wasn't quite as overrun with toys as it could have been. Interestingly, as I look back on this time, the toy rotation was more for me than for the kids. I was attached to the toys we had chosen, so rather than whittle down to the space we had, I created a system where we could store the excess and enjoy them from time to time.

Truth be told, even though I felt like I was rotating them often, I probably realistically only switched them out once or twice. The toys in the storage room were out of sight, out of mind to me until I needed to retrieve holiday decor or something else from the basement locker. I likely would not have noticed if they had altogether disappeared.

When our third baby was on the way, we moved to Austin, Texas for Dave's new job. We bought land in a suburban neighborhood and began to build a house. Unpacking all the way into a temporary apartment didn't seem smart, especially as I was very pregnant, so we kept most of our boxes in storage and lived with a minimum level of everything for the interim. One plate and fork for each of us.

Again, the boys seemed happy as could be with the small handful of three or four toys that we had out for them to play with during the six months we lived in the apartment. We spent most of our time outside, where they were always entertained. On rainy days they played pretend, ran around with towel capes tied to their backs, and invented games with some tiny plastic army men that had made the toy cut. I don't know if they noticed that the majority of their toys were gone, but if they did it didn't bother them.

Plum was born two weeks before Christmas, the same week the house was finished. We moved in on December 23rd. Rather than buying any new toys for the kids, Dave and I had hatched a plan to create a real playroom for them in the room the floor plan listed as "the office." We would decorate and fill it with all of their old toys. After six months, we figured they wouldn't remember most of them, and we needed to unpack anyway. It seemed like the perfect plan.

Christmas morning, the boys found the French doors to the playroom wrapped with paper and tied with a bow. They pushed them open to reveal a simply decorated room with a new soft rug, bookshelf filled with their old books, a couple comfy floor cushions, and two toy bins filled up with their old toys.

They were beside themselves! They happily dug through the bins, oohing and aahing as if this was the first time they had seen these things. They were once again so easy to please.

Another few years later we had another big move. Midway through The Challenge, we again packed up everything we owned and headed east, back to Virginia. Our next house would be less than half the square footage and several rooms smaller than the one we left in Texas, and I was equal parts nervous and curious how the smaller space would work with our now bigger family.

All three kids moved into the same room that also doubled as the toy room, using a bunk bed with a trundle to fit comfortably. The small room also accommodated one skinny bookshelf, the mini kitchen where Plum cooked all of her pretend meals, and a dresser for their clothes. The multiple boxes of toys we had brought from Texas once again needed some attention, and we sat down to sort them.

The toys we definitely wanted to keep went into a small basket, and everything else went into a donation bag. I moderated, helping the kids decide which toys they not only liked the idea of, but also played with often. The two small boxes of Lego stayed, as did Plum's favorite Cabbage Patch baby doll, a set of small plastic animals, one favorite Iron Man action figure, and an Etch A Sketch game.

Once again, I realized how adaptable kids can be. Their ability to play only seemed to increase even as our toy collection decreased. All three kids were happy playing with what we had, whatever that happened to be.

Through a whole year of not buying new toys, the only time I heard them complain about toys was occasionally when we were actually in a store passing the toy aisle or when they saw an ad for something new on TV. They loved the idea of having more or different toys, but it didn't actually impact them at all to not act on that desire.

This ability to focus more with less stuff doesn't only affect young kids. Teenagers and adults benefit from less stuff the same way kids do. The more clutter in our homes, the more mental energy we spend maintaining it.

The things we own have to be cleaned, organized, stored, and sometimes even used. The Pareto principle says that only 20% of our things are used 80% of the time. As we reduce the other 80% of our stuff, we only gain time, energy, and focus.

Most adults don't have bins of toys to sort through, but we all have our equivalents. Mine is a craft room full of colorful supplies ready for my next project. The problem with a full room of supplies is that I often feel distracted by it all. Where do I even begin with so many possibilities?

As I organize, donate, and reduce my craft supplies, my focus and excitement for creating increases exponentially. Just like the kids, I will use what is there so much better if what I keep is only the very best. Rather than feeling the stress of all of these unfinished projects, piles of unmet potential and undiscovered possibilities, I realize it is very freeing to simply let them go! Donate the fabric I had bought for that baby quilt and was never going to make. The baby is now in second grade, and I'd rather reserve my energy for new, exciting projects than feel the pressure of past projects not yet begun.

. . . . .

What is your hypothetical toy bin? What area of your life could benefit from more focus as you organize and reduce the stuff? As you begin making decisions about what to keep and what to let go, be aware of all of the many benefits of the latter. Letting go means freedom to live presently, meaningfully today. You will gain focus and clarity as you cut out the fringe excess and keep only what matters most and brings the most joy and value to your lives.

Choose something, and give less a try. Start with a temporary solution, and put a pile of things away in the garage or the attic for a time. See what you miss, if anything.

Life will go on happily as ever and you'll be able to breathe easier with less clutter and more focus in your home and life. That's a good feeling.

FIVE FAVORITE THINGS EXERCISE

Are you having a hard time narrowing down what to keep and what to get rid of? Try this exercise:

Consider the categories of items in your home one by one. Come up with your five very favorite things in each category. Then, move on to your next five very favorite in that category. As you actually begin prioritizing your absolute favorite things, I suspect you find you don't get very far before you realize how many items in one category you own but don't love or use.

Working from the top, down helps you to recognize and enjoy what you really have space for, or as Marie Kondo invites in her book *The Life-Changing Magic of Tidying Up* keep only the things that "spark joy." Consider donating the rest!

Some categories that I know often get cluttered up in our house that you might consider starting with are:

- ▹ Toys
- ▹ Books
- ▹ Shoes
- ▹ Jackets
- ▹ Kitchenware
- ▹ Pairs of socks
- ▹ Handbags
- ▹ Sports equipment
- ▹ Beach towels

Fill in your own five very favorites from several categories, and continue the practice as you move through your house deciding what to keep and what to purge.

_____

▷ _____
▷ _____
▷ _____
▷ _____
▷ _____

_____

▷ _____
▷ _____
▷ _____
▷ _____
▷ _____

_____

▷ _____
▷ _____
▷ _____
▷ _____
▷ _____

"Each time we asked for help, we were going out on a limb into a space of vulnerability, and learning we could trust others to care for us in a time of need. And each time they asked for help, we learned that to serve and share is to love.

Chapter 9

BUILDING COMMUNITY THROUGH BORROWING

"4:30 p.m., up Big Cottonwood Canyon. Sounds great. We'll see you there." I sent the email and closed my laptop. Our 2017 family photos were booked, and with one of my very favorite photographers. Now what were we going to wear?

In years past, this would have been immediate cause for a shopping trip. I liked our annual family photos to be coordinated, but without looking too contrived. We should be matching, but not too matching. I wrote an entire blog post dedicated to finding the perfect outfits for family pictures, to join the thousands of similar articles already available online. "Decide first on casual, semi-casual, or more formal attire." "Choose one main color and two accent colors." "How do you want the photos to feel, then choose items that feel that way."

However, this year would be a little different. Not only were we halfway through the experiment, which meant no new clothing for any of us. We also were halfway across the country, living out of suitcases while we moved from Texas to Virginia.

Dave had gotten an unexpected offer from a big company in Richmond to be one of their in-house council. We loved living in Austin, and built our home there thinking we would raise our kids to be teenagers in the Hill Country. But when the opportunity came to trade billable hours at a law firm for a more family-friendly in-house position, we took it.

In April, we accepted the offer. In May, we visited Richmond as a family for the first time, and explored what would be our new home. In June, Dave began working at his new job, while I coordinated the sale of our first home and navigated the moving company packing away everything we owned to be stored until we landed in Virginia at the end of the summer. And in July, we were sitting by the pool at my parents' house, enjoying what felt like a very normal summer vacation in a very not-normal year of change.

Because I didn't yet know any great photographers in Virginia, I booked a friend in Utah for our annual session. We took photos up the canyon in fall-ish outfits to "feel" like it was closer to Christmastime than it actually was, because I was going to use one of these portraits for our annual Christmas card. I know it may seem odd, but in my opinion, the card should reflect the season of the year when it was opened—like somehow opening a card in December of us smiling in tee shirts and sandals would make the recipient feel cold.

In short, I had lots of ideas about how to dress for family photos, and it was time to figure this year out.

I looked through the clear storage boxes that I had used to pack for each of the kids during our summer visiting family. The boxes had been storing old baby items and some never-used party supplies before our move. But, going through our belongings while packing, I had donated the contents and converted the boxes to pseudo-suitcases for easy access during our road trip and to serve as makeshift dressers at Grandma's house.

After six months of not shopping, a lot of the kids' clothes were in worn condition. Nice enough looking for playdates or even school, but not as clean and crisp as I wanted for the family picture.

There was one pair of the boys' jeans without holes in the knees. Plum had a linen dress that I had made for her for Easter that looked good enough to add to the coordinating outfits. Both boys had church shirts that would work beneath some sort of sweater.

As for me, I brought one pair of my own black jeans for the summer, which seemed silly because I was living in the same shorts and tee shirt almost daily in the Utah heat, but they would work for a portrait.

Now, what about everything else? Heading to the mall to pick up the last couple coordinating items would have been so easy. In past years, I had taken one afternoon to run store to store and grab the just-right everything. But this year I thought about my sisters, who both lived nearby and both had similar-aged children. They would have closets full of options. In fact, it might be even better than going to the store!

I quickly dialed my older sister's number and asked if I could come "shop her closets" for our photo. She agreed and told me to bring the kids to play while I was there. Fifteen minutes later, the kids were all playing downstairs in her basement with cousins while we sat on the floor of her bedroom pulling sweaters and dresses out of the closet for me to try on.

We chatted and laughed, catching up on the day's antics as moms. She told me some stories I hadn't heard before about the ongoing intertwined relationships of her longtime book club friends, and also about her long-distance bicycle training.

I shared all my plans for settling into Virginia the following month, and got her up to date on our no-shopping challenge. Wandering through her kids' rooms together, she pulled out sweaters and shirts, pants without holes, and even fresh socks. Her youngest daughter had a cardigan that would go great over Plum's dress. Both of her sons had things that would fit my boys just right. We even grabbed a pair of pants and shoes from her husband's closet for Dave to wear in the photos.

I left with my arms piled high with options, and my heart all filled up from spending some time with family. On the way home, I called one of my other sisters and asked to borrow a flat-brimmed hat, the very last thing I wanted for the pictures.

We swung by her house on the way back to Grandma's to pick it up, and the next day we donned our outfits for the session. Hat-to-boots borrowed clothing that was matching, but not too matching—and coordinated, but not too contrived.

As we smiled and cuddled and posed for the camera, I felt my love grow for this little family, and gratitude for capturing another year of growing and learning together. I also looked around at our fresh sweaters and shiny boots and felt connected to my larger family, who had participated in our photos by generously sharing their clothing with us.

We could have just as easily taken photos in our tee shirts and holey jeans—and I'm sure we would have loved them—but I appreciated the feeling of accomplishment that came from both not buying new things AND creating the experience we hoped for.

. . . . .

During this year of no shopping, we weren't on an island. When we wanted something to use temporarily, there were more options than either buy it or go without. We also had the option to borrow from friends or family, and invite others to help us along the way. In fact, the idea of borrowing was one that I really liked as we had brainstormed possible obstacles to navigate when embarking on The Challenge.

We have always been lucky to have great neighbors, and to know them well. It didn't happen by accident either. When we were newly married and living in a small apartment outside of Washington, DC while Dave attended law school, when our first neighbor moved out soon after we arrived and we knew the apartment was available, we found another young family looking for housing to move in next door. "We could trade babysitting and co-op Sunday dinners!" we exclaimed. And then sweetened the deal by offering to return the $250 referral fee that the apartment complex gave us back to them. We were serious about choosing great neighbors.

Sharing meals, toys, walls, and even internet access with our neighbors created a deep and lasting friendship. We felt needed and supported even though we lived thousands of miles from family of our own. When one family was out of eggs, the other was sure to have some. When the printer was out of ink—no problem, the other is full. We shared spaces, belongings, time, and even children, swapping babysitting for date nights and hands-free grocery trips. I felt certain that living in community was the way life was meant to be. The word "community," after all, stems from the word "common" which denotes sharing or collective ownership.

When that family moved away, we wasted no time filling the spot with another wonderful family we knew. While we kept in close touch with our first neighbor-friends, we settled into common living with new neighbors. More shared meals, more traded favors. With each knock of the door and exchange of time, energy, support, and cup of milk, we deepened our roots to this place, and to each other. These were healthy friendships, as close as family relationships, that felt like home away from home.

In those years, we learned to use borrowing and sharing as a tool for creating connection and relationships. Each time we asked for help, we were going out on a limb into a space of vulnerability, and learning we could trust others to care for us in a time of need. And each time they asked for help, we learned that to serve and share is to love.

In a world where so many people feel alone, we felt surrounded and supported because we didn't try to do life on our own. We invited and actively participated in creating deep and meaningful friendships one knock on the door at a time.

We had grown quite adept at finding amazing neighbors, and this continued when we moved to Austin, Texas. We built our house on a piece of land outside the city. It was a cul-de-sac, half-acre lot, with a grove of twisted live oak trees and access to a hundred acres of wilderness preserve. After growing our family to five in under 900 square feet, it felt like time to stretch out our wings a little bit.

Although we had searched for a charming old fixer-upper house closer to town, we fell hard for the lot and the neighborhood. The local school and involved church congregation also drew us in tightly, so we signed the dotted line to build our own house.

A new friend, who we had met at church the first Sunday in town, was also house hunting. She was surprised when I confirmed our new build. After all, in one of our first conversations we had connected over our love of older homes in established areas, with their big trees and oozing charm.

"Come see!" I told her. "There is a lot next door to ours that is still available and I think you'll love it!" She laughed and said maybe they would swing by.

A year later we once again had best friends for neighbors, and we were spending Saturdays sharing a porch swing and Mondays trading decorating tips. When our homes were both finished we had six children between us, who were growing up spending as much time together as if cousins, and some weeks maybe more like siblings.

Being so close, both in proximity and in friendship, we decided to go in on a lawn mower together. Each family would only need to use it once per week in the growing season, and sharing both cost and maintenance seemed like a good idea. (In reality, we probably only used it countable times, because our family regularly neglected our lawn care, which made the arrangement even more beneficial for the neighbors we shared with.)

I borrowed their table saw to finish DIY projects. My neighbor, being afraid to use the saw herself, borrowed my sawing skills to make the cuts she needed for her own projects.

Beyond sharing and borrowing, there was support and bolstering. The relationship grew as we reached out for help and stepped up to return it. Over the years, our community extended far beyond our besties next door into other neighbors, families at our school, friends in business, and members of our congregation.

Maybe it was through years of developing confidence in our ability to ask and receive help—in many forms—from our community, that we felt the transition into not buying anything new might be easily navigated during our experiment. We knew if there was something we really needed, we could borrow it, rather than buy our own. In fact, it was a skill we had been practicing for years, with all positive results.

Even though the main principles of the experiment were to practice gratitude for what we already had, and to practice patience waiting for things we didn't, a side benefit of borrowing was that we deepened our community ties without having to buy or wait. We weren't on an island where all we brought in the suitcase was all we could use. Inviting others to participate along the way through small favors and simple sharing brought an air of community to the effort and enriched our year with deeper relationships and closer friends.

There are so many things we own but don't use often: books we only read once then retire to a shelf, formal dresses we buy for a wedding and then hang in the back of the closet, power tools that come in handy during a big project then sit collecting dust in the shed. What if we considered sharing more often? What if we could use what we needed when we needed it, and let others use it at other times? What if our relationships could deepen and our community could increase through the repeated connections that come in asking for and returning simple favors?

INTERACTIVE BORROWING LIST

Write a list of as many items as you can think of that are unique (not a lot of people might own them) and not used often (it wouldn't affect your regular life for someone to borrow it). Invite a couple other close friends and family members to do the same. Exchange your list with people you feel comfortable with, and build up your community by creating an interactive borrowing/sharing list.

You might have a chainsaw your friend could use to chop firewood, and someone else has a snow-cone maker you could borrow for your daughter's upcoming birthday party.

Before making a big purchase for something you might only use once or twice, consider sending around a text message to a few people, asking to borrow one. Not only will you save money, space, and time not shopping, but you will create a small connection with another person. That is what it's really all about, anyway.

THINGS I COULD LEND   THINGS I SHOULD BORROW

_____   _____

_____   _____

_____   _____

_____   _____

"
Truly, you have to make
the decision to eliminate
unnecessary decisions.
It doesn't happen
on its own.

Chapter 10

CAPSULE WARDROBE AND UNNECESSARY DECISIONS

The elementary school pick-up doors were a hub of neighborhood activity. Each afternoon moms and dads, nannies and grandmas wandered over from their houses tucked conveniently into the blocks surrounding the large brick building. We chatted and waited for the bell to ring and our little ones to emerge, bursting with energy, from a day learning and playing inside.

Today I had Plum in the stroller, and our excitable new puppy Quincy on the leash. The walk to the school was one solid piece of our daily routine. In fact, although my life was filled with twirling unknowns—frequent, new contracts for my freelance work as a blogger; spontaneous weekend trips I would throw together when the weather looked good; last-second dinner parties just because I wanted to entertain our friends and loved hosting—the regular hum of day-to-day life had become comfortably, cozily systematic.

I woke up at six-thirty, changed into exercise clothes, and woke up the kids. We made scrambled eggs and toast, packed backpacks, and walked six blocks to the school. Plum went to a nearby preschool couple days a week, but on the other days, she would join me in my drive to meet my friends at the local YMCA for Body Pump exercise class. She walked right into the kids' corner, excited to play with friends, and I would head back to the wide room at the end of the hallway where the class met at 8:30 a.m.

Whichever of my friends arrived first would set up benches and retrieve weights and the bars for the others. We always congregated on the left side of the room, near the front but not the very first row. Then, once everyone arrived and the music began, we lunged and lifted along with the beat. Each song as familiar as childhood lullabies, drilled into our heads and bodies through months of regular attendance. We would sweat and smile, grateful to have a regular exercise routine that included friends. No one really had to decide whether or not to go, it was just what we did.

After class, I took Plum home to play with toys or watch a show while I quickly showered and got dressed. This, too, was an easy regular routine. My closet in our new home was as big as a bedroom had been in any of our apartments, but the hanging bars held just a handful of shirts, sweaters, and dresses. My daily uniform was simple: skinny, high-waisted jeans, a soft tee shirt or loose button-up, and flats.

Over the past few years I had simplified my wardrobe down to the most essential pieces. Things that fit my body, fit my style, and fit my budget. I had at some point realized that I was spending a lot of time and energy wading through a closet full of clothes I didn't like, trying to find an outfit that was inspiring or unique. These days, emboldened by The Challenge, and the months of experiences guiding me towards a simplified lifestyle, I didn't need a unique outfit every day.

Years before I might have been embarrassed about wearing the same clothes over and over again. I remembered a time when we were newly married that I tried to keep track of which dress I had worn to church for weeks on end, so as not to repeat too soon. As my life became more and more full of things that really mattered to me, like creating thoughtful DIY projects, developing and fostering friendships, and being present for my children and husband, I realized I didn't need to spend any extra time or energy on not repeating outfits. I just needed to put on clothes I liked, that made me feel comfortable. That turned out to be a lot easier than I had been making it.

Downsizing and editing my closet had not only reduced the time and energy I spent getting dressed every day. It had also increased my confidence. Once I made the decisions about what clothing worked for me, I saw my own style and choices as independent of the whims of fashion trends. As The Challenge began, I had deleted emails from my favorite clothing stores, edited my social media following to include only people who uplifted and inspired me, and stopped going into clothing stores completely. Then, I simply got dressed every day in clothes I loved.

Today, I had grabbed the usual: black skinny jeans with small holes worn naturally through the knees, a teal-colored cotton v-neck tee shirt with a pocket on the front, and my old Converse sneakers. I wore the same jewelry that I had for years, dainty gold pieces that felt like extensions of my own body. I blow-dried my hair, brushed a little bronzer onto my cheeks, donned a flat-brimmed hat, and checked my watch. We had time for a quick trip to the dog park before lunch, nap time, and picking the boys up from school.

While Plum napped, I had finished some work projects. A styled photoshoot of an outdoor reading nook I had built was due to the company, and I needed to finish editing the shots. I also returned a couple emails, then swept and mopped the wood floors (which I always did on Thursdays during nap time—it was part of the schedule).

As we walked in the sunshine to the school doors, I laughed at the puppy scampering along by the wheels of the stroller. Plum was enchanted with this new little fur-ball of a sister. It was a beautiful, regular day.

We arrived a few minutes before the bell rang, and one of the neighborhood moms waved hello. She was a friend from church and we saw each other almost every day. Today, she looked me up and down and asked, "Miranda, how do you always look so cute? I swear every time I see you, I think you are dressed so well. Where do you shop? I need some new clothes and love what you wear."

I smiled, a little baffled. "Thank you! You're so nice!" I said. "Honestly, I wear the same things almost every day. Skinny jeans and a tee shirt!" I went on to tell her about my edited closet and how I literally mixed and matched the same clothing in different combinations, but it wasn't science or art. It was simple. She was intrigued and said she wanted to try it, because she was really so impressed with the way I dressed. "Give it a try!" I laughed. "You might love it!"

As the boys and I walked home, I thought a little bit more about the exchange. I had probably received more compliments about my wardrobe in the five months that I had stopped shopping completely than in the whole rest of my life. In these months that I had deliberately stepped out of the race of dressing to impress, I had found a new type of confidence and ease that must say more than a simple outfit could. Less daily decisions meant more energy management and convenience, and also spilled over and showed up in added confidence, creativity, and contentment. My outfits hadn't changed but thanks to The Challenge something inside of them had shifted. By focusing my energy on what felt essential in my life, I was at peace with myself and that was the new energy others could feel.

. . . . .

When we were first married, Dave and I frequented home stores to gather supplies for our first small apartment. We needed pillows, curtains, a bathmat, and a bunch of other little odds and ends for daily life. But as soon as we stepped foot inside the warehouse, I would be immediately distracted by the huge selection of every type of home good available. So much so that I couldn't focus, much less make a decision. And I'm usually a very decisive person.

On my way to the towels section of the store, I'd get stuck looking at toothbrush holders. Heading toward vacuum bags, a display of perfect spatulas would catch my attention. This type of shopping provided me with so many stimuli that my mind would bounce about thinking of all of the possibilities for all of these things that I wasn't even aware of, much less in need of.

What I didn't realize then, was that all of those unnecessary decisions were wearing me out inside. Our brains can only handle a certain number of decisions per day before we start to lose self-control and willpower. This drain on our brains is called "decision fatigue," and most of us experience it without even knowing what it is.

One way to conserve more energy for decisions that matter most is to spend less energy on decisions that don't matter very much. To spend less energy, you can tuck a few choices nicely into a routine, and not think of them again.

Some examples are: creating a meal plan, setting days of the week to complete different household tasks, shopping at only a couple favorite stores that align with your style and budget, and operating with a wardrobe made up of only your favorite clothing.

Before The Challenge, I had already chosen a couple areas in my life to create a basic pattern and eliminate unnecessary variety: scheduling my household tasks, creating a regular exercise plan, and making the same simple meals for my family every week. One of my very favorites was building a capsule wardrobe to decrease my fashion decisions into a manageable group of favorite clothing items.

If you have ever packed for vacation, you have in some small way created a capsule wardrobe. You chose a few things that will mix and match well together, and you packed it all into a suitcase for the trip. You don't pack your entire closet, but stick to a smaller subset of clothing for a specific amount of time.

A "capsule" is simply something encapsulated into a small, contained space. Like a capsule of medication. You may also remember the popular "time capsules" of your childhood. Everyone chose something special to close up into a box and not open again until some future time. It was a snapshot of one particular moment in time. (I think my family did one in 2000 that we have never reopened!)

Capsule wardrobes use the same idea. They are small, intentional, contained wardrobes. You make some deliberate choices about which essential clothing items you want to use for the next season, then don't add to it for a certain amount of time, usually one season.

The idea of a capsule wardrobe emerged in London in the 1970s when Susie Faux, owner of the boutique "Wardrobe," introduced a collection of essential clothing items that wouldn't go out of style and could be mixed and matched.

Then, in 1985, Donna Karan introduced her Seven Easy Pieces fashion collection. In this landmark collection, the models began in black tights and bodysuits, then layered the other seven pieces of the collection in different combinations to make up the entire show.

Right now, capsule wardrobes are trending. Because of the trendiness, there are so many different people sharing about their own capsule wardrobes, and they all vary a bit. Some fashion bloggers buy a whole seasonal "capsule" of the latest clothing, mix and match it for a couple months, then buy a whole other "capsule" for the following season. This isn't the type of capsule I use and such a method doesn't necessarily hold to the original principles of a capsule wardrobe: containing essential pieces and making them last.

A capsule wardrobe eliminates the need to use precious energy to think about what you wear. You choose which favorite pieces you want to include in your closet. Every day, you can pull anything off of the shelves and hangers, knowing it fits, looks good, and you like it. That's an amazing feeling!

As soon as you have it all assembled, you spend a couple months mixing and matching from your closet until the new season. Or, if you live in the mild Texas weather, like I did, you could use the same capsule wardrobe for a whole year!

The initial building of a capsule wardrobe looks a lot like a basic closet cleanup. Take everything out of your closet. Try it all on. Ask yourself: What fits? What doesn't? What are you keeping around for sentimental reasons rather than necessity? By the end, you have chosen your very favorite clothing and shoes, made sure everything fits well and looks good, and you no longer have to make those same choices every morning as you try to get dressed.

When I started using a capsule wardrobe, I realized I had essentially been doing it already, just without getting rid of the other clothes in my closet. I was automatically reaching for the same clothes over and over again. I always pulled on those favorite jeans, and that great, cozy tee shirt. I was avoiding things that I didn't like or that didn't fit well.

When I pared down to the forty or so items that I actually loved, wore often, and was comfortable in, I felt more myself in my clothes than I had for years. It made me realize how much happier I am when my closet has a very edited, deliberate, selection of high-quality clothes that I love.

. . . . .

I can't believe how much unnecessary time and energy I used to put into trying to create innovative outfits every day, or make sure I didn't wear the same thing too often. I've now simply embraced that I love to wear the same few things that make me happy and not think about it anymore.

Not only has simplifying the decisions in my closet minimized the energy I spend dressing, but also shopping. Considering thoughtfully which items of clothing I owned and wanted to wear often made my personal style pretty clear, and it helped me see which brands of clothing I love and that truly lasted.

I began using a capsule wardrobe a couple years before we began The Challenge. When I looked ahead at a year of not shopping, not buying clothing didn't feel like much of a problem because I was already keeping a very intentional closet. What I didn't realize was how quickly some of my often-worn favorites would wear all the way out!

During those twelve months of The Challenge, I walked straight through two pairs of shoes. My old Converse had already been on their last legs when we began the year, and by November the holes were all the way through both soles. The leather ankle booties that I wore daily from January to April turned out to also have been worn through the sole when I pulled them back on in the fall. I spent half the day with a sopping wet sock when I ventured out on errands without realizing the cracks in the rubber went all the way inside the shoes. They were all used up, and used up well.

My kids also wore their clothes out to completion. Every pair of pants had holes in the knees by the end of the spring. A quick snip of my sewing shears converted them all into shorts for the summer that should have lasted through the end of the year.

Our move to the colder climate of Virginia necessitated one trip to the store to pick up small, intentional capsule wardrobes for the kids in the new cold weather. We chose three pairs of pants, three long-sleeved shirts, and a jacket for each child. They could use their current clothing to mix and match in the rest.

Creating small, intentional wardrobes for my kids was another great way to eliminate decision making and gain back some time and energy. They had enough clothing to wear for a week. They could mix and match whatever they chose each day, and all of the options worked.

Choosing ahead to only have items in our closets that we

loved, that fit, and that we were willing to wear over and over again, made the morning routine so much easier. I could tell the kids, "Put on whatever you want!" and be confident with the outcome. And I could tell myself the same thing, "Put on whatever you want!" and feel confident and comfortable in my clothing every day.

Truly, you have to make the decision to eliminate unnecessary decisions. It doesn't happen on its own. Billions of marketing dollars are spent to present you with the question "Do you want one of these?" You have to fight to ignore those questions and preserve your decision-making energy.

. . . . .

Here are some strategies I use to preserve my decision-making energy: I toss out clothing catalogs before poring over the pages; I delete solicitous emails before filling my hypothetical shopping cart; and I edit the marketing messages I receive on social media by unfollowing people or brands who are constantly enticing me to spend, shop, or compare. These days, I don't even go into stores without a specific reason and a list.

I don't need marketers to tell me what I need. Being present in my everyday life is enough to inform me of my actual needs. Without constantly being distracted by the new, shiny, beautiful world filled with more, I can reclaim the power of living my life to the fullest. I can leave everything else in the stores without even having to consider if I might want it.

The counterintuitive reality of consciously narrowing my options during The Challenge is that, rather than feeling restricted, I feel so much more free! My mind has space to think creatively and openly about how to approach tricky situations with the kids, or what fun sewing project I'd like to work on.

Maybe clothing *IS* your thing, and thinking through all of the possibilities in a full wardrobe and picking out amazing new outfits daily is what boosts you up. That's wonderful! Just make sure you save yourself enough energy to do it. Is there something else you could simplify for happiness?

Maybe it's what you eat for breakfast, or what you gift for birthdays, or which shampoo you use. Think about what the unnecessary decisions are in your life that you could simplify for sanity and happiness.

More choices are not always better. Continually making these decisions can begin to deplete your energy rather than conserve and boost it. Some choices can be made into routine so that they become background music for the beautiful, more important decisions and journeys of our life.

DECISION ELIMINATION:
MAKING SOME CHOICES HABIT

Consider some of the decisions you make every single day. I'll bet a lot of them are the same. What time to wake up, what to eat for breakfast, what to wear. When to do the dishes, when to take your lunch break, when to go to sleep.

Maybe some of the answers to these questions are already habits for you. Maybe you can think of a few more specific to your life that you wish were already routine.

These questions, along with hundreds of others, fill our lives and drain our energy. Which can you choose to eliminate? Give this some thought, and choose three routine decisions to automate for a simplified life.

Maybe you want to put the dishes into the dishwasher every morning before work. Maybe you want to wear pink on Wednesdays. Maybe you want to go to bed at ten o'clock. Make the decision, write it down here, and let it go!

1. _____

2. _____

3. _____

"
Part of what I love about
the openness in a room
is the possibility. That
space allows some rest
for the mind, and in
turn invites creativity
and inspiration.

Chapter 11

THE VALUE OF SPACE

Spring had begun in a burst of wildflowers along the highway. Waves of indigo bluebonnets danced in the breeze as Dave and I drove downtown for our weekly date night. We pulled into the parking lot at Contigo, my favorite local restaurant in Austin.

This farmhouse burger and spicy fried green beans had been one of the reasons I fell in love with this city so quickly, and now after four amazing years, we were saying goodbye.

We were initially drawn to Texas for the heat, and the space. Dave's job as an attorney in a DC-area law firm required long, intense hours, and we were all ready for a chance to clean the slate and begin anew. He settled right into the more laid-back culture of the Austin law firm, and I settled right into designing a brand-new house.

The suburban neighborhood and brand-new ranch-style home was just what we had been looking for—blocks away from a great elementary school, nestled into a community filled with kids riding bikes and swimming on the local swim team.

In seven years of marriage, we had only lived in small apartments in the city, and the idea of stretching our legs on some land felt incredible. We felt like we had made it! The new house was four bedrooms, and three bathrooms, with an open concept kitchen, playroom, covered back patio, and a two-car garage. What more could we need?

On the day we moved in, I held our ten-day-old daughter in my arms, and watched our two rambunctious boys running through the echoing halls. I thought to myself, "I will never take this space for granted. This home for our family is all we have ever wanted."

And it was. It was cozy and homey and lovely. In the beginning, it was also empty. We had nowhere near the furniture needed to fill the rooms. So we started collecting. Through Craigslist, outlet stores, and DIY projects, I designed each room with intention. Year over year, the rooms became layered with colors and textures, art and plants.

The open shelves and closets gave way to boxes and bins. Baskets and bottles slowly filled the cabinets in the bathroom. Stuff in stacks piled up, ever so neatly, on the laundry room counter. The two-car garage fit two cars, then one, then none at all.

After four years of living in the beautiful new house, I realized that so much of the space we had initially chosen was gone. We had covered it up with stuff! It was this realization that prompted The More Than Enough Stuff Challenge. I knew that even if I organized and purged and donated, we would only stop filling space when we stopped buying more.

Maybe it was fate that sent Dave that email invitation to apply for a new position across the country. Maybe it was fate that I sent him off to the interview, telling myself it was a good chance to "keep his interviewing skills sharp." Maybe it was fate that washed over us with unexpected excitement when the offer came and we said "Yes!"

I had never imagined we would be packing up and moving out so soon after we each pressed our hands into the wet concrete of the driveway. Those five hands cemented into the ground were now left for curious future owners who might wonder about the family who had built and loved this house, and then moved away.

Somehow, mixed in with all of the sadness of leaving a place we had loved so dearly, was a twinkle of enthusiasm for this opportunity to change. We loved the moments and memories made in this first home. And I already knew the next one would be different.

Our initial months of The Challenge had reminded me how little we need to be happy. I could reflect back over our life and see that the common thread of happiness, contentment, love, and peace had very little to do with our circumstances and everything to do with our intention.

The Challenge had allowed us to take ourselves off of the hamster wheel of more, bigger, and better. I had opened my eyes to the way we had been caught up in following the classic pathway to generally accepted success in America: Go to school, get a job, have a family, buy a house. The only logical next step was: "buy a bigger house." Except, that wasn't the plan.

"How do you feel about moving into a smaller house?" I asked Dave, as I dipped my crispy green bean into Contigo's spicy aioli.

"What do you mean?" he asked, seeing that familiar twinkle in my eye.

"I was thinking that when we move to Richmond, we should rent a small house for a year while we look for something to buy. We have already reset our shopping habit, maybe we could reset our 'bigger is better' mentality too? Plus, it would be temporary! Another experiment within our experiment."

"Sounds fun," Dave laughed. "What have we got to lose? Let's do it."

We finished off our burgers, enjoying the breeze and twinkle lights of the outdoor patio as we discussed possibilities, details, and dreams for the next chapter of our life in Virginia. It was going to be amazing. I already could feel it.

. . . . .

In the month of July, after seven months of not buying things, we had everything we owned packed onto a moving truck headed east. A couple months earlier, during our house-hunting trip to Richmond, we had signed the lease on a 1000 square foot rental house near the city. This was less than half the square footage of our home in Texas, and we felt great about it.

While we prepared to look for the rental, I had spent a lot of time considering what amount of space our family actually used. I would close my eyes and imagine the floor plan of our single-story rancher. In my head, I could envision it as a heat map, with each of my kids as a glowing light, moving through from the front door back to the kitchen, into the yard, and back into the kitchen. They took occasional trips into the playroom, and of course occupied their beds in bedrooms at night.

In my visual heat map, there were entire rooms in our house that were rarely used at all. All five of us spent the great majority of the time in the open concept kitchen living room. This is where we ate and played games, read stories, and watched movies.

The backyard area came in second-most used. The kids would run out daily to the trampoline or shoot Nerf guns at the fence. I spent a lot of time when the kids were at school in my home studio office, working or sewing. This exercise also taught me that no one ever spent any extra time in the laundry room. It was really only where we washed and dried the clothes. The folding and organizing all happened in the living room in front of the TV.

The garage was useful for storage, and occasionally for parking cars. But I could easily see that we needed and used far less space than we actually owned. The decision to downsize seemed obvious.

We moved out of our Texas house in July, but didn't settle into Richmond until the end of August. Our summertime routine included a long road trip through Utah and Arizona to visit friends and spend time with cousins and grandparents, and this summer was no different. We stayed between our families' homes, cabins, second homes, and even on the houseboat during our summer vacation. And it was a really interesting study in space. All along the way, I was taking mental notes of what we loved, what we used, and how we lived in each different place. These ideas helped inform my decisions about what we might be looking for in our next house. It was exciting to give ourselves time and space to make a different choice than what might be obvious: another big house in the burbs.

One place that we loved spending the night was in my parents' vacation home in Southern Utah. Not only is the home thoughtfully and beautifully designed, but it is intentionally minimal.

Of course, a second home naturally doesn't have all of the years of storage, books, boxes, clothes, furniture, and stuff that collects in any normal home. And that is part of what we loved about it! The empty space in the closets and corners was such a breath of fresh air.

When we were there, I remembered how much I liked space. Not necessarily square footage, but just a little empty space within a house. I remember thinking, "We could live like this. We could have more space even with fewer square feet. We could create an escape in our own home."

Part of what I love about the openness in a room is the possibility. That space allows some rest for the mind, and in turn invites creativity and inspiration. Eliminating all of the unnecessary in our surroundings can also quiet the clutter in our brains.

Going to sleep and waking up peacefully in a house filled with so much space, I realized I could make our lives feel slower and more simple by just paring down. That open space begins to emerge naturally when you get rid of things that you think you have to manage simply because you own them.

When we first arrived at my mother-in-law's home in Utah, she was excited to show us the garage. The space had formerly been the catch-all for leftover furniture, goods, boxes, storage, and the stuff. It had been piled high from their last move, and she had emptied and organized the whole place for Father's Day, so her husband could park his car in the garage.

She told me she sold the furniture online, went through and donated most of what was in boxes, and didn't miss a single thing she had gotten rid of! She also said exactly what I had been thinking and feeling: "I think we forget how valuable it is to have empty space. The space is worth more than the stuff."

. . . . .

So why do most of us have more stuff and less space? Why do we imagine that by filling up our homes we'll feel all filled up?

I think anyone who has ever organized a cabinet or "dejunked" a closet can remember that sigh of relief when there was once again some space. But then we turn around and pile it in and on again and again.

It may be human nature to always be looking for more. Perhaps it is a survival mechanism. But what about having more room to rest, more time to play, and more ease in cleaning and organizing because everything has a place with some room in between?

After months and months of focusing on loving what we had, eliminating things we didn't love, and intentionally not buying anything consumable to add to our closets or shelves, I was convinced that freedom and contentment were positive byproducts of simplifying. Open space feels like freedom to me!

Do you think much about the space that surrounds you in your homes and lives? The space that you fill up, empty out, organize, and reorganize? Do you realize that empty space is an incredibly underrated asset?

We tend to value the stuff that goes into the spaces more than the space itself, which is why we find ourselves with bulging closets and cupboards. More clothes than hangers and books than shelves.

Once the space is full, it isn't really space anymore. We have removed all of the benefits of having a little breathing room. The possibilities. The rest for our eyes, arms, washing machines, and wallets.

Moving into a smaller house in the middle of our year of less helped me learn to create open space, even within a smaller house. It didn't begin that way, though.

The day we moved into our 1000 square foot, two-bedroom, one-bathroom rental, the movers had to pile things in the front and back yards because our belongings literally did not fit within the walls of the home. I had done my best to minimize before the move, and had grossly underestimated how much we actually owned. It all seemed so small when it was behind a closet door!

Imagine everything you own sitting in a pile in the front yard. If you had the chance to take things inside, one-by-one, and put them back into your house, what would you choose? What would you leave behind?

I walked through this real-life exercise, with the new neighbors wondering what was happening. After taking several loads of chairs, rugs, books, and clothing to the donation center, I could actually begin focusing on organizing the space within the walls of the house.

Because this home was temporary, and we weren't yet sure what the next house would be, I put some very favorite furniture, camping gear, holiday decor, and piles of boxes from my sewing room into a storage unit. We arranged all three kids into one bedroom, and Dave and I in the other. Each room had a bed, dresser, rug, and bookshelf.

I put a couch and coffee table into the living room, with a small desk in the corner for the computer. We moved our small table and chairs into the kitchen and a small pile of clean towels into the one linen closet. And that was about it!

This house was less than half the size of our house before, but we used it just as well. We had space to snuggle up and read together. We had space to sit around the dinner table.

We had chosen to not fill the entire house up with our things, so that we could instead fill it up with feelings of peace and contentment, joy and love.

Undoing my ideas about how big or full a house has to be helped me remember the purpose of a house in the first place: to provide shelter and safety for my family. It was a place where we could learn and grow together.

Dramatically downsizing both our house and our belongings during our cross-country move proved to accelerate my understanding that we already had all we needed to be happy. We didn't have to continue trying to fill up our space, or ourselves, with things we didn't need. We could leave some space to grow. Leave some space to rest. Leave some space to breathe. And leave some space to live.

CREATE SPACE EXERCISE

Choose one area in your home that you would like some more space.

Take everything down or out, and sort by type.

Ask yourself the questions:

- ▷ Do I love this item?
- ▷ Do I use this item often?
- ▷ If I was in a store today, would I buy this again for full price?
- ▷ If this item was sitting in a giant pile in my front yard, would I choose to bring it back inside?

Sell, donate, or otherwise discard the items that don't make the cut.

Then, as you put them back, leave some space. If there is a shelf in the closet with nothing on it, let it be. When you stack your books back onto the bookshelf, see if you can leave some room to breathe on one side or the other.

Challenge yourself to remove something from every surface in your home. Chances are, most things that are sitting out have no purpose, and you will find you feel lighter and happier, more content and peaceful when they are gone.

. . . .

PART FOUR

MORE ADVENTURE

"We stopped
adding stuff
to our life, and
instead added
more life to
our life.

Chapter 12

IT'S NOT ABOUT
THE MONEY

My cell phone buzzed on the counter. "$400 RT tickets to London, let's book a girls' trip!" The text message from my globe-trotting older sister made me laugh. I could count on Chelsea to be on the lookout for a trip any day of the week.

Her budget and stamina for vacations has always exceeded mine, and the last two times she had casually mentioned a quick trip to Europe I had politely declined. I enjoyed living vicariously as she made the hops across the pond without me, but also really wanted to join the fun.

This time, instead of an immediate no, I stopped to consider some of the changes we had made during the last several months.

In not buying non-consumable goods, we had started to have a soft cushion in our budget. Our move to Virginia and decision to downsize into a small rental house had also freed up some extra money each month. Considering those factors, and the airline vouchers Dave had just received from being bumped on a business flight, I thought it could work.

"Let me check with Dave. Sounds so fun!" I shot back, and dialed my husband's office.

We decided to visit London, Paris and Amsterdam over a long weekend in the fall, spending a couple days in each city to absorb the sights. My older sister Chelsea, younger sister Emmy, Mom and I wandered beautiful alleys, oohed and aahed over the architecture and design. The baby sister of the family, Mattie, was on a study abroad in Italy, enjoying a concurrent European experience. (My dad and two brothers were used to us girls taking off on quick adventures and were unfazed.)

London was as bustling as I remembered it. I had been once before, in high school, and loved the red buses, black cabs, blue uniforms, and grey sky. We hauled our luggage up the narrow stairway to a flat nearby Piccadilly Circus, which wasn't actually a circus (!) at all, then headed out to explore the town.

In forty-eight hours we visited Buckingham Palace, toured an exhibit of the late Princess Diana's dresses, cheered through a musical, and enjoyed tea time in the trendy pink basement of Sketch London. We ate and walked and laughed through the city, soaking in as many good bits as we could before hopping on the train to France.

Paris was our shortest stop. We had one day, and it was one amazing day. Our rented apartment in Le Marais district had massive picture windows that opened onto a cobblestone street. French flags from the building across the way fluttered in the friendly morning air while we dressed and mapped our plan for the day.

We ate flaky baguettes from a boulangerie on the corner, then walked to the River Seine where we rented bicycles for the day.

Rather than fight crowds at the Louvre, we studied Monet's Water Lilies up close in L'Orangerie and wandered through the Tuileries Garden. We filled the afternoon with cruising down narrow streets to visit all of the shops on our list, delighting in crepes, then chocolate, then rich cheese fondue.

Someone had brought a boom box to the park across from the Eiffel Tower, and we couldn't stop giggling as we took turns capturing the most perfectly Instagramable portraits possible. Along with a hundred other strangers all jamming to the soundtrack of Daddy Yankee singing "Despacito." The sun set on our one magical day in Paris and it felt like the most wonderfully full day I could remember. We slept, then headed north to the Netherlands.

Steps off the plane we came face to face with hundreds of bicycles stacked on racks. The statistic we had heard about there being more bikes than people in the city of Amsterdam now seemed believable. On a boat ride through the historic canals, I fell instantly in love with the Dutch Canal house style. Tall, narrow facades with steep gables and layers of lean windows. The black, deep green, and dark blue homes especially struck me as unique and beautiful. My head was spinning with design inspiration.

We spent the final two days of our European adventure sipping mint tea while we ate overstuffed apple pie, wandering beside foggy windmills, visiting the hidden rooms where Anne Frank wrote her diaries, and experiencing Van Gogh up close. One afternoon, as I walked along the sea shore in Marken, breeze gently blowing my hair and sunshine beating down on my face, I thought how trading some stuff for experiences like this was a decision I would make a hundred times over.

. . . . .

You may think that in not shopping for a year, we saved a nice nest egg. In fact, saving money wasn't a main purpose of our experiment. We weren't concerned with saving money. Don't get me wrong, if you want to save money, not buying things is a great place to begin. The amount you save will be dependent on the amount you currently spend on non-consumable goods, and for some people that is a lot! For us, it was enough that I started to notice a small cushion of extra money in the budget each month, and rather than saying "yes" to new things on a regular basis, I began to say "yes" to more adventures. Trips to the museum, trying that new restaurant downtown, packing up for a quick weekend away. We stopped adding stuff to our life, and instead added more life to our life.

Saving extra money is often a really good idea, however when we focus so much on putting money in the bank, sometimes we forget about what money is good for. How it can be spent to enrich our lives with experiences and memories that shape our perspectives and build our relationships. I learned about money from a young age and was encouraged to budget and save and save and save. While I understood having some money set aside for a rainy day and to prepare for the future, I couldn't help but feel like at least some of my money should be used on things that brought me excitement and fun into my life as a kid, and then a teen, and then a young married, and then a young mom. If it all is stored away for the future, when exactly is the future?

From the time I was a teenager, I always had a job and worked hard to earn money. I also had a very clear earning, saving, and spending cycle. I would choose a destination, work long hours and sacrifice weekends to save enough money for a trip, then spend all of my money on the trip, and start over again. Some of the most inspiring times of my life were spent abroad, learning about other cultures and connecting to the wider world.

When I was nineteen, I spent ten days backpacking in the jungle of Costa Rica with two girlfriends. I had lived in the area for a study abroad, and wanted to return to experience more of the rugged culture. We slept in tents on the beaches, hiked into a biology research center, and spotted a wild crocodile, eyelash viper, and herd of coati along the path.

As a twenty-two-year-old, recently returned from eighteen months of formal missionary service in Buenos Aires, Argentina, I decided to save money for a service expedition to Bolivia. Much like the trip I had taken as a teen to Mexico, but this time without my family along. I spent a week in the high Andes, learning phrases in Quechua to supplement my fluent Spanish so I could converse with the villagers in their brightly colored skirts and long black braids knotted on top of their heads.

When I graduated from nursing school, Dave and I took a month to backpack around Thailand. We lived on under ten dollars a day for a month, sleeping in hostels, eating incredible street food, and feeling so tiny in the big, wide world.

I remember thinking to myself often as I was buying a plane ticket for a new adventure: "I can always earn more money." And that was that! I saw money as a renewable resource that enabled me to live the life that I desired. What a freeing concept! What a difference from the paralyzing scarcity mentality that often surrounds finances. Money is energy, and when we develop a positive relationship with it, often it flows more easily into our lives.

All of that said, Dave and I have had many lean years. We were married as college students, and scraped by during his graduate studies with my part-time salary and a lot of resourcefulness. Even after our years of schooling were finished, we maintained a fairly specific budget. The variable spending category included consumable goods like groceries and gas as well as non-consumable goods like clothing and furniture. When we stopped buying non-consumable goods there was a little more money left to spend in different ways. As when I was younger, I defaulted to experiences and adventures. I could say "yes" more often to going and doing rather than simply acquiring.

. . . . .

As a society, we can easily become caught up in the idea that more money equals more happiness. We believe that a few more zeros at the end of our paycheck will offer us the life we really want, and then are surprised when that big bonus doesn't actually solve any of our problems.

Although it is hard to believe, once your basic needs are met, having more money doesn't increase happiness, yet we still all chase more money, prioritize more money, and even measure our self-worth by the size of our bank account. But, you know what does increase happiness? Having new and exciting experiences with people you love. Taking that trip, seeing that play, enjoying that new restaurant, crushing your kids on the mini golf course.

Choosing to spend money on experiences with our family, often and intentionally, has been one of the biggest positive lifestyle changes we have made. We always had been adventurous, and tried to make little things happen here and there. Now, planning those experiences is an even higher priority. I know that saying "yes" to spending money on a family vacation may mean saying "no" to a new couch this quarter, or putting a wardrobe update on pause for a while. I also know that, for us, it is worth it.

I can't imagine looking back on my life and wishing I had more money in the bank, or bought more clothes or owned newer cars. I will remember the time I spent with my husband and kids, the adventures that taught me about different cultures and connected me to the world, the ways I was able to add value to other people's lives, and enjoy my own.

SAVE TO SPEND EXERCISE

Sometimes we get so caught up in the idea of saving money for saving's sake, we forget that money by itself is neutral. It is only good for what we use it, and I believe one of the most meaningful ways to use it is on experiences with family and friends.

List three experiences you have been dreaming of. Choose one that is small, under $100, one that is medium, under $700, and a large experience of over $700. These desires gain power when you acknowledge them and write them down!

_____ $_____

_____ $_____

_____ $_____

Determine how much money you might need for each of them and write a budget next to each experience.

Now, for the next few weeks or months, take money you would have spent on unnecessary stuff (like new clothes, toys, or decor) and put it aside towards one of these experiences.

Naturally, you will save the money for the smaller experience first. When you have saved it, USE it! Take your kids to the movies, go to a live concert. Exchange the money you might use on something you won't remember for an experience that becomes part of who you are.

"Receive
with gratitude
and give
with love.

Chapter 13

GIVING AND RECEIVING GIFTS

My kids were giddy with excitement over the visit of Mamo and Papa (as we lovingly refer to my parents). As soon as they walked in the door the kids bounced around them, asking if they had brought surprises, as they did every time they visited. Right on cue my mom unzipped her suitcase and began pulling out gifts.

Mamo first unveiled a sweetly embroidered Mexican dress for Plum. It was a souvenir from her recent travels. She had also brought a beautiful woven Mexican fabric for me, and some treats and games for the boys. As I watched the kids run back to their rooms with their new prizes, giggling over their good luck, I quickly realized that I had not taken gifts from others into account when planning our guidelines for The Challenge. In the one month since we began, we had not bought anything for ourselves, but what would we do when others bought things for us?

Of course I couldn't refuse the gifts. The kids were so excited, and my parents were so generous. Scrambling in my head to figure out how to handle this unforeseen dilemma, I decided maybe we would be able to maintain our experiment by calling the gifts replacements. We would donate one of Plum's old dresses and a few of the boys' toys in order to maintain at least our base level of stuff. Part of the point was to not acquire more, and this way, at the very least, we would maintain.

I felt pretty good about this adjustment to our guidelines. We could accept gifts, as long as we donated a similar-type item so we weren't continually acquiring new stuff. Of course, we wouldn't be seeking gifts out. No calling my sister to ask her to please mail me that thing that I wanted so I could call it a gift. (I won't say the thought didn't briefly cross my mind.)

The following night we lined the benches in the small gym at the local YMCA. After the boys had expressed interest in basketball, we signed them both up for local teams and were cheering wildly as they ran back and forth across the court. It was especially fun to have Mamo and Papa in town to experience the games. We have lived away from our families since before any of our children were born. Having them around for something like a weeknight basketball game felt super special. I was grateful for their visit.

A couple days later, while pulling out of the garage, I noticed a stack of Amazon boxes on the front porch. That blue smile on cardboard was recognizable from across the driveway. It was a familiar, exciting feeling to see a package at the door. Yet, I hadn't made an order. And I wasn't expecting anything.

· The kids ran over excitedly and each pulled open one of the three cardboard boxes. One by one they each revealed a brand-new basketball. One per child, in each of their favorite colors.

The familiar smell of new rubber made me a little dizzy, and I caught my mom's smile from the corner of my eye. "Well, you didn't buy them," she said slyly.

I couldn't help but be excited for the kids as I watched them dribble down the driveway, then dash across the cul-de-sac to practice shooting. The neighbors had a hoop in their driveway and my kids made themselves at home tossing their balls wildly toward the backboard.

I didn't blame my mom and her thoughtful gifts. Here was something we could use to spend quality time together, and encourage the kids to continue developing their talents. These new toys didn't necessarily distract from our relationships, and rather looked like they would add to them.

Now I was in another quandary. I hadn't bought the toys myself, so technically I was still living within the guidelines of our experiment. But the acquisition of more things during a time when we were earnestly focusing on using what we already have was a paradox.

I felt a little like a hypocrite, as silly as that is. I really want to live with less, organize and reduce what we own, and love more fully what remains. Getting more wasn't part of the plan.

· · · · ·

These very first gifts during our More Than Enough Stuff Challenge opened up a question that we hadn't fully considered when we began. What would we do when friends or family gave us gifts? We could control the gifts we chose to give each other as a family. We had already outlined that we would either give gifts of experiences or create handmade items using materials we had on hand.

My mom's quiet and well-meaning generosity reminded me that we cannot control the gifts that are given to us. How could we remain true to The Challenge, and our minimalist goals and ideals, during the year while still being gracious and grateful?

Because gratitude was one of the focuses of The Challenge, it was easy to see that we would receive gifts with gratitude and grace. Gifts are an expression of an emotion and a way to bind relationships. Often, the giver of the gift receives more satisfaction and joy than the recipient. We didn't want to deny our friends and family members the opportunity to feel that good will and love that comes with gift giving. Still, there had to be something we could do when we received unexpected gifts to still maintain our minimal mindset, and practice the art of not accumulating more.

As I was pondering on how to find that balance between receiving gifts without constant accumulation, I spotted the abandoned Amazon boxes that had been filled with basketballs. They were the types of cardboard boxes that I often used when I was cleaning out a closet or decluttering a cabinet. Suddenly, a light bulb switched on. I would fill the box with the items that were still in good condition, that I no longer needed or used, and deliver them to a donation center.

This seemed like a perfect solution to creating a system where we could both receive gifts with gratitude and grace, and also not fill our drawers to overflowing. With each gift we received, we would turn around and give something away. Those cardboard boxes or holiday gift bags would be a reminder to find a couple things in our house that we weren't using anymore, and donate them to someone who could.

As the kids ran back inside, sweaty and happy from playing basketball, I invited them to walk through the house with me, picking out items that we no longer needed. Things that were still in great shape and could be loved and appreciated by someone new. In thirty minutes we had filled both boxes with books, boots, table linens, wooden blocks, kitchen items, and a few kids' clothes. Stuff we would not miss, and that someone else would love. We would receive, and we would give.

It seemed like a good system. We would not buy new things on our own. When we received gifts, we would turn around and give away equal or greater quantities. Receive with gratitude and give with love.

Okay, okay, now that I was thinking about it, I had some new questions about receiving gifts as part of The Challenge. What about swag? As a blogger, this was something I knew that I would deal with regularly. Part of my job involves partnering with companies to feature products that we love—and those products are given to me as gifts in addition to the money I make from the collaborations. I wasn't sure exactly how I would navigate it all, just that I wanted to stay true to the principles of gratitude, abundance, and love.

While my mom stayed to watch my kids, I hopped on a plane to attend the first big blogging conference of the year. I usually attend two or three, and my goal is to connect with potential sponsors and also with other bloggers and influencers to help each other promote small businesses or new projects. Upon check-in I was given a giant box of swag. The consumables of chapstick, candy, and a little bottle of lotion I tucked into my purse, and decided to offer the non-consumable towel, water bottle, socks, and necklace to my roommates rather than taking them home. These weren't really personal gifts, and I already had more than enough at home.

Later that day, I was congratulating a friend on the launch of her new, fully customizable planner company Golden Coil.

Her kickstarter was just about to launch, and she told me she would love to send me one as part of the promotion, as a gift.

I'm embarrassed all over again to report that I told her that I already had a planner for the year, and had just begun this challenge to not add more stuff this year. Unfortunately, I wouldn't need one of her new ones.

Ouch. No gratitude. No love. No grace.

I was a little unprepared, and a little self-righteous, not to mention awkward, insensitive, and unintentionally unkind. I was thrilled for her new venture, thought the customizable planner idea was genius! I quickly emailed my friend: "Of course I would love to try out your new planner!" Both to better organize my life, as well as to support her in her endeavors.

This brought up another question. How could I support and encourage my friends in their business endeavors while still not actively adding stuff to my life? I'm still not totally sure, but I know the solution there lands in much more gratitude, acceptance, and flexibility than I offered in that moment.

I could accept gifts with gratitude, then turn around and give with love. Say yes to friends with small businesses, projects, and products they hope I can help promote. Not seek them out, but say yes to gifts when they feel personal, appropriate, and authentic. Also, I could continue to be generous with what I give (and re-gift). I would love to be able to extend some of these lovely items and experiences to friends and family around me who will be thrilled with the swag, the stuff, and the love.

While I was away at the conference, my mom added a basketball hoop to our driveway, stocked the kids up with a couple new outfits, and after I took her to the airport, I discovered new swimsuits that she had tucked into the top of the boys' closet. I don't think she understood our goal with The Challenge, and I am still very grateful for her generosity and love.

The practice of giving gifts may be as old as humankind itself, with symbolism laced through every culture, religion, and government. Gifts are symbols of love, peace, and partnership. Cultures and families have developed their own gift-giving traditions, and in every country and society there is some form of gift giving embedded in the lives of the people. I love to give gifts, and have always found such joy in finding or making the perfect item for a friend or family member. And, that joy of giving is universal.

As we say, "It is better to give, than to receive." Rather than try to stop people from giving us gifts, and in turn rob them of some of the fun of giving, we may do better to receive with gratitude. Once we have expressed love and appreciation for the items, there is no reason we have to keep them, especially if they don't add value to our lives. Donating or finding a friend who would actually love and use them may be a good option.

I also found that as I shared about The Challenge with friends and family, the gifts we received during the year seemed to be more in line with what we would use. One thoughtful friend brought me a couple bottles of my favorite dish soap, another took me to the movies. Gifts can take so many forms, and in stepping outside of the traditional gift guides, we might find some new ways to give and receive gifts that are better than before.

What about birthdays and holidays? More and more people are hoping for a meaningful, magical, minimal holiday without all of the stuff, expense, overwhelm, distraction, and general

discontent that can come with such high commercial expectations set by...well, everyone.

Have you ever sat and watched kids open gifts on Christmas
morning, and they take one look, toss the item, and ask for
more? That whole more, more, more experience takes away so
much from the ability to process, enjoy, and feel grateful for
receiving something. It feeds the feeling of discontent, and there
is nothing more sad than kids sitting surrounded by their piles
of gifts, feeling bad for themselves.

We have taken a minimal approach to Christmas, even before
The Challenge. When Dave and I were first married, we made a
point to discuss how we wanted to handle the holiday season,
knowing we had come from quite different backgrounds and had
different family traditions. We talked about which Christmases
had been our most memorable as kids, and what we felt were
the most important traditions to include, and then made some
guidelines for ourselves to make it easy every year.

Perhaps not surprisingly, our favorite Christmases were not
the ones we received a pile of fancy presents. They were the
years our parents had created unique experiences for us to enjoy.

I remember one year opening up a tire on Christmas morning, while my sister opened a steering wheel, and a brother
opened a helmet. We were a little confused until my dad led us
down to the driveway where there was a little red go-kart for
our family to enjoy! We cruised that thing all over the neighborhood for a few years, taking turns driving and riding. It was so
fun, thoughtful, and intentional.

Once Dave and I started having our own kids, I was even more
grateful we had created some guidelines. It is so so easy to be

swept away by the glossy catalogs, trimmed-out shopping malls, and basically the messaging of the entire season that is "If you buy these things you will have a better, happier Christmas!"

The pressure to buy big, glamorous, expensive gifts during the holidays is ever present, and sometimes we can feel like our love is measured by how much we spend or how big the box is. But all of that focus on materialism takes away from the real joy of the season, and can leave more than our wallets feeling empty. In contrast, when we spend our holidays focused on togetherness, spending time and fostering real connection, we find ourselves all filled up by the season.

We have been able to make our family Christmas so meaning-ful and magical, even staying true to our Christmastime values of family, togetherness, gratitude, and celebration of Christ.

The guidelines we chose all those years ago are still the ones we use today, and that served us well during The Challenge year. Let me share them with you:

FAMILY THEME

Santa will give gifts along a family theme, and they will always be something we can do or experience together. We want to cultivate a feeling of love, recreation, and family enjoyment with the gifts that the kids wake up to on Christmas morning, rather than have them each get a toy that takes them off to play on their own.

Some examples of this from our family are: everyone get-ting a sleeping bag and headlamp, then we all went camping together; each of the kids getting a wooden swing to hang in the trees in our backyard where they could all play together;

the whole family getting a Madsen Bucket Bike filled with a few Nerf guns, so we could ride and play together.

Additional ideas we have for the future include: a year where everyone gets tennis rackets and lessons, a whole round of new bicycles or scooters (on a year they also need them) with matching Anderson Bike Gang tee shirts, or backpacks packed with snacks and travel goodies and an airplane ticket for a weekend family getaway.

During The Challenge last year, Santa filled our stockings with consumable goods including coloring books and markers, stickers, and a few sweet treats. Then, instead of receiving individual gifts from Santa, the kids found a note that sent them on a scavenger hunt. At each hiding spot, they found a clue and a different consumable treat all leading them back to a big wrapped box addressed to the family. They opened it up to reveal a long paper chain counting the days until Spring Break with tickets for a family adventure in Italy! In our family, Santa is all about family togetherness, and during our no-shopping Christmas, rather than traditional gifts, we decided to have him invest in a family adventure, instead.

GIFTS FOR DEVELOPMENT AND IMAGINATION

We as parents will choose one special gift that encourages growth and development. These gifts are usually more like what they would put on their Christmas lists. A new, cool Lego set, or a special baby in a stroller. The key here is choosing one thing and sticking with it. Kids, like adults, are easily overwhelmed by a deluge of stuff and too many gifts ultimately leads to distraction and disappointment.

USEFUL STOCKING STUFFERS

We fill stockings with useful things and treats. Dave grew up with an orange and a box of mini cereal in his stocking, mine were usually stuffed with jewelry, makeup, DVDs, and maybe a camera. So, we had different expectations.

I love stockings as a way to give some fun, and practical things that the kids will like and also need. Cute socks, maybe new mittens or a beanie (if we need them). We still do the mini cereal for nostalgia, and also include one of those plastic candy canes with the candy inside because our kids think they're the most wonderful things. The last couple years I've also included a family-friendly DVD for us to watch on road trips or Friday movie nights. Simple, useful things.

If you come from a maximal Christmas background, the idea of only two or three gifts under the tree sounds ludicrous. "You are depriving your kids of the experience of having their dreams come true on Christmas morning," you might say. If my kids' dreams stem from opening a bunch of random toys, I hope to adjust our family experience to reflect different values.

We want our kids to be celebrated and doted on as much as the next people, and we decided way back before they came that the best day for the royal treatment is on their birthday! The day that is celebrated only because they were born.

With these simple guidelines, we've been able to navigate and create magical, minimal Christmases without feeling over-whelmed, overindulgent, or disappointed. We brainstorm gift ideas by asking the question "What new family experiences would we like to have this year?" and are unaffected by the catalogs and sales of the season. We set ourselves up for success by choosing what matters most, and sticking to it.

BIRTHDAYS AND OTHER GIFT-GIVING HOLIDAYS

For other gift-giving holidays during The Challenge, we focused on giving non-material gifts, or gifts of experience. My oldest asked for a membership to an online math game that he had played at school for his birthday. In addition, I wrote him a handful of "Experience Coupons" that he could use at his leisure during the year. They were things like "Go on a date with mom," "Stay up 2 hours past bedtime," and "Invite 3 friends over for ice cream sundaes." We made the day feel extra special by decorating the house with banners and balloons, eating delicious meals, and of course enjoying a birthday cake.

Since we weren't buying toys for any of the kids all year long, I helped each of the kids plan a fun birthday party. We knew that their friends would bring gifts, and decided ahead of time that we would encourage the kids to accept them with gratitude. Then, they could decide on a few older toys to donate after the party to make room for their new ones.

The simple mentality of accept and give, versus accept and acquire, made such a difference as we navigated the holidays during The Challenge. Holding lightly to our belongings meant it was easier to donate and organize and reduce the stuff, even when we received new things from friends and family on occasion. Practicing the art of choosing rather than simply mindlessly allowing the influx of stuff helped us to be more intentional about what we use, keep, and want to carry with us throughout our life.

How do you think about gifts? Do you love them and then tuck them away and forget about them? Do you feel pressure to keep anything that has been gifted to you? More even than things you have chosen for yourself? Throughout The Challenge, I returned over and over to the idea that we must choose what fits into our lives, and what does not. Without making decisions about what we want to own and care for, we will be slowly buried in our belongings.

Even when you are on board with the idea of less stuff, gifts may cause some hang-up for you because of the sentimental nature of them. It has been helpful for me to remember these couple principles when considering gifts others give me.

1. THE GIFT IS ONLY A REPRESENTATION OF THE EMOTION OR RELATIONSHIP.

Just as when you buy things, you are usually buying a feeling. When someone gives you a gift, they are actually expressing an emotion. Maybe it is love, maybe gratitude. Maybe some gifts reflect admiration and hope for a deeper relationship. From time to time, someone may give you a gift to express control or power. Regardless of the gift itself, the emotion is what is being given. And, if the item that is given doesn't fit into your life at some point, that does not mean the emotion or the relationship is no longer valid.

You can donate that crystal bowl Aunt Sarah gave you for your wedding without meaning any disrespect to Aunt Sarah. In fact, when you are thoughtful about curating your belongings, it actually allows you even more time and energy to spend on the relationships that matter most!

2. YOU CAN'T CONTROL HOW GIFTS ARE RECEIVED.

When you give a gift, your responsibility for that item ends when the gift has been delivered. It is not your job, nor your right to expect anything in return. Whether or not the gift is received with gratitude and love or rejection, you did your part in the giving. That is where your participation in that exchange can end.

So often, people give gifts with so many strings attached that the gift is actually like a ticking bomb of expectations. Is that really a gift you want to give? I have friends who dig old trinkets out of storage every time their mother-in-law comes to visit, so they can have the gifts she has given them over the years on display. This entanglement of expectation and emotion with things they don't even like feels like a lot of wasted energy.

I have decided that when I give someone a gift, part of my gift will be the full release of expectations regarding what they do with it. They can love or hate it, keep or donate it, thank me or not mention it. I get to feel all of the love and appreciation as I choose and give the gift, and that is all I have to feel.

If you have a hard time letting go of your expectations surrounding gifts you give, I suggest you consider examining those feelings and choosing to spend your precious energy elsewhere!

3. GIFTS OF EXPERIENCE ARE THE VERY BEST KIND OF GIFTS.

If we give gifts to convey some sort of emotion and build relationships, what better gifts can we give than those that invite more quality time and meaningful interaction? Gifts of experience do just that. Rather than another physical item, a gift of experience is a gift that shares an opportunity for a moment, an adventure, or a memory. Most of my very favorite gifts that I remember were gifts of experience.

Gifts of experience usually include tickets to an event, lesson, or getaway. They can also be coupons for special time spent together. During The Challenge, all of the gifts we gave to each other within our own family were gifts of experience. These included: a membership to an online game, tickets to a go-kart race, movie passes, concert tickets, gift cards for ice cream, a weekend trip to our favorite getaway, and for Christmas, a family trip to Italy.

The things that you give will eventually be used up or worn out, but the experiences you give will bring you closer together as you create memories that enrich your family forever.

50 GIFTS OF EXPERIENCE

You may love the idea of giving gifts of experience, but have no idea where to begin! I've included this list of 50 gifts of experience to give you a starting place. As you start choosing experience gifts, you will find some that you really love, and want to give over and over again. (I give away movie passes and manicure gift cards a lot!) You will also get to know what types of experiences you and your family and friends really enjoy doing together and be able to seek those out specifically. For example, Dave loves stand-up comedy, so I know if I can get tickets to a great comedy show he will really love them (versus tickets to a Broadway musical—which is what he can get for me!).

. . . . .

1. CAFE GIFT CARD
2. ICE CREAM SHOP GIFT CARD
3. COUPON FOR A HIKE
4. HOMEMADE PICNIC
5. ROLLER SKATING RINK PASS
6. GARDENING CLASS
7. LOCAL MUSEUM TICKETS
8. MOVIE TICKETS
9. BOWLING VOUCHER
10. IMPROV COMEDY SHOW TICKETS
11. ARCADE GIFT CARD
12. DRIVING RANGE PASS
13. LASER TAG OR MINI GOLF PASS
14. ROCK CLIMBING GYM PASS
15. FERMENTATION WORKSHOP
16. CAMPGROUND FOR THE WEEKEND
17. TRAMPOLINE PARK PASS
18. ESCAPE ROOM TICKETS
19. YOGA PASSES FOR A MONTH
20. THEATRE TICKETS
21. CONCERT TICKETS
22. FAVORITE RESTAURANT GIFT CARD
23. TICKETS TO A SPORTING EVENT
24. THEME PARK PASS
25. DANCE LESSONS
26. SPA PASS
27. CLEANING SERVICE FOR A MONTH

28. MANICURE SERVICE

29. MUSIC CLASSES

30. KAYAK OR CANOE RENTAL

31. POTTERY CLASSES

32. COOKING CLASSES

33. AQUARIUM PASS

34. SKYDIVING ADVENTURE

35. HOTEL STAY

36. OPERA TICKETS

37. ART STUDIO CLASS PASS

38. CHEESE TASTING

39. PHOTOGRAPHY CLASS

40. LOCAL CITY SEGWAY TOUR

41. FLOWER SHOP GIFT CARD

42. HOT AIR BALLOON RIDE

43. CYCLING TOUR

44. NATIONAL PARK PASS

45. CHEF'S TASTING MENU

46. LANGUAGE CLASSES

47. GAME SHOW TICKETS

48. PHOTO SESSION WITH PHOTOGRAPHER

49. AIRLINE VOUCHER

50. WEEKEND VACATION

"
You gain all of the value,
inspiration, and benefits
of creativity regardless
of the outcome. So, if
you choose to create,
that is enough.

Chapter 14

CREATIVITY IN MINIMALISM

From the moment Milo emerged from the school's swinging side door, he didn't stop talking. Pokémon cards in hand, he excitedly rambled about this character and his special powers, and that card with its valuable hologram. He was in second grade, and Pokémon was all the rage. Luckily, he had amassed quite a collection of cards before The Challenge began, and our guidelines allowed him to spend money he earned doing chores or for his birthday on whatever he liked. Usually, that was more Pokémon.

During the five-block walk from the elementary school to our house, I pushed Plum in the stroller, held Eliot's hand, and listened to Milo chatter enthusiastically about the successful trades he had made at recess. As we rounded the cul-de-sac on final approach to our front door, he announced that he had everything he needed for Pokémon cards, except for a binder.

"What is a Pokémon binder?" I asked, still a few steps behind this new craze. Milo explained it was a three-ring binder, like a school binder, but with clear sleeves inside that held each of the cards individually. That way, rather than sorting through a thick stack of cards to find the one you were willing to offer up in trade, you could simply flip through the pages and see all of the fronts and backs of the cards easily.

"Mom, everyone else has a binder, and I really need one!" he commented. "Can we run to Target and get one? It won't be expensive."

Hmm, a binder for Pokémon cards. This would be an interesting creative challenge to face without buying anything new.

We were several weeks into The Challenge, and had already had many make-it-work moments. For example, just days after we officially began not shopping for non-consumable goods, my younger son, Eliot, had declared he wanted a new toy car and could we please make one with supplies from my in-home studio. I had jumped at the chance to show him how we could employ supplies we already owned to fill wants or needs that we had during this year-long experiment.

Eliot and I had pulled out modeling clay, tooth picks, wire, acrylic paint, and brushes from my overflowing craft closet. We spent an hour shaping and smoothing the clay before letting it dry into a tiny car. Milo and Plum had been equally excited for the chance to craft with Mom, so in addition to a car, I had helped mold a miniature motorcycle for Milo, with Plum happily "helping" on my lap.

We took a break and had a snack while the clay air-dried. Round two of craft time involved painting the wheels and bodies of the vehicles. Milo chose black paint, and added a tiny bolt of lightning to the side of his motorcycle. Eliot wanted his car to be bright red, with black and silver wheels.

The experience of making the toys was a win-win situation. Not only were we not buying new, unnecessary toys. We were also spending quality creative time together! All four of us felt more connected to each other at the end of the project. We also felt more empowered in this new journey to use what we had in new ways.

I had no shortage of craft supplies, but my office supplies weren't quite as robust. Especially after I had recently organized the office cupboards and purged anything that I couldn't see a use for. Milo's Pokémon binder was a new type of make-it-work moment.

"Let's see what we have at home that could work for your binder!" I chirped, as the kids hung their backpacks on the rack and lined up at the counter for an after-school snack. "I'm sure we have something that will work well."

I filled water cups and smeared cream cheese on toasted bagels while I reviewed in my head options that might work for a card binder. There were a couple three-ring binders of recipes in the pantry that I could condense into one, freeing up a blank binder for the cards. But what about the clear plastic sleeves?

While the kids ate, I brainstormed ideas: I could tape a few Ziploc bags together and hole-punch the edge. That wouldn't be super stable, but it would do the job. Maybe I use the extra whole-sheet plastic sleeves floating in the back of my high school scrapbook? If I added some double sided tape to the inside of each sleeve, it would separate off sections for the individual cards.

Thinking about my old scrapbooks reminded me that Dave had a box of his childhood memorabilia in the closet as well. I knew he had collected baseball and basketball cards, maybe he had just what we needed?

Inside Dave's box of memories we found a couple cardboard boxes of baseball cards, and some photos and journals. A little deeper, I discovered what we were looking for! His baseball card binder, complete with pages and pages of plastic sleeves all lined with batters and baseman, frozen in their caps and cleats.

I called Dave at the office before dismantling the collection. "Hey honey, Milo would love to put his Pokémon cards into a binder to make trading with friends at recess easier. I have been trying to make that happen with things we already own, and I found your old baseball collection binder. Would it be okay if we use a few of those pages for Milo? I'll tuck the cards we remove back into one of the boxes, so you can figure out what you want to do with them later."

Dave just laughed. "Of course you can use those! I didn't even remember I had kept those cards. I'm excited to see what you all put together! And it will also be fun to show the kids my baseball cards tonight when I get home."

We hung up the phone and Milo and I went to work gently removing baseball cards from the sleeves and then filling them back up with the brightly colored Pokémon characters. He beamed as we snapped the rings closed, all of his cards contained safely within his new binder.

The last step was to find some fun Pokémon clipart to print and slide into the clear, plastic sleeves on the outside of the plain white binder to make it official. Milo loved looking through the pages of illustrations on google image search and choosing a couple that he thought were super cool. When we finished, he spent the few remaining minutes before dinner time showing Eliot and Plum all of his most powerful and valuable cards, flipping happily through the pages of his new homemade Pokémon binder.

"I had no idea how well equipped we were to handle this challenge," I thought as I watched the kids huddled together on the couch. A month before I would have driven the kids to Target to pick out a binder, and moved on with life. It might have seemed easier or more convenient, but we would have missed out on this whole afternoon of problem solving, and creativity. We would never have remembered the baseball cards, or given Dave a chance to help out and feel part of the adventure of the day.

Sometimes convenience is overrated. Creativity is empowering and inspires connection and confidence. I was excited to continue down this path of choosing to be thoughtful, intentional, and creative as we lived the life of creativity over consumption.

. . . . .

I've always loved figuring out how to make things work. Back in the early years when Dave and I were recently married, we had no money, and no extra space in our 400 square foot apartment. We made holiday decorations from printer paper, Christmas ornaments from ginger bread, and borrowed (a lot of) things from our friends and family when needed. We felt completely, utterly happy. We were filled with joy, adventure, creativity, and love. We had everything we needed, and were so content.

Our lean years lasted a long time. After I finished nursing school, we moved back east to work through law school. The apartments stayed very small, and the budget was even smaller. We became experts at making do and being resourceful.

One year, I began a custom sewing business to earn a little money in addition to my part-time RN salary. We were living in the DC area and I noticed that there were lots of opportunities to sew custom costumes and clothing for people on Etsy. Knowing that it would be much easier for me to work if my sewing machine was already set up somewhere, I converted the 15 square foot coat closet of our apartment into a makeshift sewing studio. It was the only place in the apartment where I would be able to close the door when I wasn't working. With a curious toddler underfoot during the day, I needed to keep the needles, scissors, and piles of works-in-progress out of sight.

Dave's aunt, who lived nearby, gave us a small IKEA desk

she no longer needed, and it fit perfectly between the wall of the closet and the door frame. I set up my sewing machine and serger on the table, then duct-taped a power strip to the leg of the desk where both machines could be easily plugged in. The other end of the power strip reached outside of the closet and just made it to the nearest outlet.

Before I began working, I would plug this cord into the wall, powering everything inside the closet. When I was finished for the day, I would gently unplug the cord and tuck it into beneath the desk. That way the doors closed completely and I could lock the closet for the night.

I hung clear-plastic shoe storage onto each of the closet doors to hold thread, supplies, and sewing notions. A few small adhesive mirrors hung on the wall behind the machines reflected the living room behind me, so I didn't feel like I was facing into a cave.

During nap times and after bedtime I would open those closet doors and enter a world of possibility. I dreamed up princess costumes and designed baby Batman suits. When an old friend saw my work on my blog, she reached out to order a custom-designed and handmade wedding gown. I excitedly agreed, and over the next couple months spent my free time elbow-deep in silk and lace.

This was the second custom wedding gown I had made. I designed and created the first before I was married. It was con-structed from start to finish on the dining room table at my parents' house. I then flew it to Mexico where I did the final fitting with one of my best friends just an hour before she walked down the sandy beach to become a wife. Gratefully, it fit perfectly.

When I wasn't sewing custom projects for pay, I was busy whipping up unique refashions for myself. I accepted hand-me-downs from neighbors and converted them into new articles of clothing. Two large, men's dress shirts pieced together easily into a small women's dress. I transformed a frumpy cardigan into a ruffle-front sweater set. Dave's old University sweatshirt converted easily into a kid-sized hoodie for the boys to represent Dad's school.

I looked at old clothing simply as cloth—able to be shaped and changed into something different than what it was. Exercising creativity in place of consumption was just a part of my life. Using what we had was the only way we knew how to live.

Even on a lean budget in a busy phase of life, we rarely felt a lack of resources. We saw our lives filled with abundance. I didn't learn to buy holiday decorations or multiple sets of dishes or shoes, because we simply didn't have the space to store them. We lived minimalism out of necessity. If it didn't fit in the cupboard or budget it wasn't welcome. We made things work because we had to.

By the time of The Challenge, I longed to return to the feeling of creativity and empowerment that came through making it work. When we had been given an inch of prosperity, we had run a mile down the road of mindless consumerism, comparison, perfectionism, and trying to keep up with what everyone else seemed to be doing.

I wanted to provide my growing kids a chance to sit down and use the talent and materials we already had to make life special. They needed to learn, like I had, that we could be happy and creative in any circumstance.

· · · · ·

The desire to create is innate to the human spirit. The way we pursue this desire varies from the obvious world of handicraft and handmade products to the more subtle creations of a thoughtfully decorated home, fruitful garden, or the ability to make others smile through creating an environment of kindness. Ask yourself: "What do I like to create?"

Anytime you act upon an idea, you are creating. And far too often, you don't act! You think about the things you would like to create, and often instead of creating, you consume. You want to write in a journal, and instead you scroll through Instagram. You want to learn to watercolor, instead you browse online. You want to build a business, and so you listen to a hundred podcasts and read a hundred books, and absorb everyone else's ideas about the why and how and where and when. Still, at the end of the day, what have you created?

Exercising creativity improves lives. The type of creative exercise doesn't seem to matter as much as the simple act of doing something creative. Do something! Anything! Doodle in the margins of your planner, try a new recipe, build a fort with your kids from blankets and couch cushions!

In our hyper-connected world, it is easy to consume all day long, every day. You consume other people's lives through social media, other people's stories through the news and television, other people's ideas through podcasts and books, not to mention all of the endless products in all of the stores all around us.

You could potentially spend your entire life always consuming, never creating. But you can't consume when you create.

These two actions don't happen simultaneously. The act of creation allows the opportunity to simply turn off and ignore those incoming messages for a while. Then, in the space and silence, you get to make your own!

Whether you choose to share your creations or not, the process of creating something makes space for mindfulness, focus, and inspiration. Taking the time to create rather than consume will stimulate your imagination, connect you to your intuition, build your problem solving skills, and reduce your anxiety and stress as it encourages you to live in the moment.

You know why I think so many people don't create things? They fear imperfection. They think making something that isn't a brilliant masterpiece would be a waste of time, and so they go on with their lives without learning what absolute joy it can be to throw aside perfection and simply make.

Here's the thing: we aren't perfect, so our creations won't be. And that is okay!

I have been making things for as long as I can remember, and not one of them has turned out exactly the way I first imagined. In fact, some of my very favorite projects through the years have been those that took on a life of their own as I made them. And because as I made them, they taught me.

Creativity is a process of learning, growing, and changing. It is an experiment. You aren't expected to be perfect. You aren't even expected to be good! You gain all of the value, inspiration, and benefits of creativity regardless of the outcome. So, if you choose to create, that is enough.

During The Challenge, we quickly discovered that creativity is a necessary skill of having less. Choosing to pause consumption automatically invites creativity back into life. It took a little extra thought to use what we had rather than continually adding more. But, when we start to see the things we have as enough, we begin to use them in different, interesting ways. We chose to "make it do" and the ingenuity we found within ourselves was inspiring.

Not only is creativity required for using the things you already have in a more interesting way, it is actually cultivated through that practice. When you exercise your creativity, it grows.

CREATE SOMETHING

Sit down today and make something using materials you already have on hand. It can be anything! As you put your creativity into practice, you will begin to grow your ability to recognize the potential in all of the things around you.

Here are a few ideas you could start with:

- ▷ Write a journal using paper and a pencil you have in a drawer at your home.
- ▷ Pull out your sewing machine and sew a pillowcase using fabric from your stash.
- ▷ Paint a picture or pattern into a notebook.
- ▷ Build a tower as tall as you can using regular household objects.
- ▷ Download a coloring page from the internet (or draw your own) and spend some time coloring.
- ▷ Arrange some flowers or branches from your yard into a centerpiece.

- ◊ Do a one-line doodle by not lifting your pen from the page while you draw.
- ◊ Bake something delicious with ingredients from your kitchen.
- ◊ Invite a friend over to make homemade pizzas for dinner.
- ◊ Mix flour and salt into homemade play dough and mold it into your favorite animal.
- ◊ Whistle a happy tune.
- ◊ Strum your favorite song on the guitar.

. . . . .

Challenge yourself to spend at least 10–15 minutes per day making something. Remember that it won't be perfect, and it may not even be good. Even if it is terrible, and you don't ever show it to anyone, you will benefit from spending that time and energy creating rather than consuming something ready-made. As you work on your creation, you will continue to build your patience, investing into the process, and gaining so much more value along the way.

"
Maybe there is
a more effective
way to feel better
than hitting the
newest sale.

Chapter 15

SELF CARE VS. RETAIL THERAPY

was ready for a break. From the moment I opened my eyes, I had been rushing between seemingly mundane tasks. Getting the kids dressed, fed, and out the door to school was a feat of great magnitude, especially if someone didn't have clean socks or had lost a shoe.

Once they were dropped off with a hug and kiss, I returned home to a mountain of laundry that needed to be washed, folded, and put away. I worked on getting loads through the wash while I checked my inbox.

There were reminders and requests, plus a bunch of the latest sales from stores that I had somehow missed when I unsubscribed from as many solicitations as possible. In a year of not shopping, it helped to not be reminded daily of all of the things on clearance.

I replied to the emails that required some thought, then pulled another load from the dryer. After a couple hours of juggling home and work tasks, I drove to the library to return our borrowed books. Except for the one we had lost somehow. Twelve dollars later my library account was cleared. I guess I had technically bought that book, but figured it didn't count as a purchase since we didn't know where it was.

Before I knew it, or felt like I had accomplished much, it was time to pick kids up from school and head to piano practice. The two younger kids and I sat in the car while the oldest reluctantly went inside for his lesson, pouting about how he didn't like playing the piano. For forty minutes I listened to Winnie the Pooh on the backseat DVD player intermixed with bursts of "He hit me!" and "I can't see the show!" We were all having one of those days.

A couple hours later, I breathed out a sigh of relief as Dave walked in the door from work. Dinner was almost ready and I planned to eat with the family then take off and leave him to handle bedtime. It had been a long day, and I needed a little alone time to relax and recover. With the dishes in the sink and kids kissed goodnight, I hopped into my minivan and turned up the radio. Singing loudly to Lady Gaga as I turned out of the driveway, I wondered where I should go.

A few months prior, the obvious choice would have been to visit a favorite store to wander and indulge in a little retail therapy. Seeing all of the new displays and finding a perfect new decor item had always felt like a great way to unwind. But now, I was taking a break from shopping for the year. Aimlessly wandering a store seemed like unnecessary temptation at best and torture at worst.

Instead, I headed downtown with the resolve to go on a walk at one of my favorite sculpture gardens instead of through the aisles of Target. I could be inspired without buying anything, and get a little fresh air while I was at it.

Near the entrance to the museum, an impressive 100-foot-tall man, fashioned of aluminum and steel, welcomed guests. Down across the bridge there was an installation of a giant wooden nest woven through the trees. It felt paradoxically otherworldly and so natural in the landscape, as if it had always been there. Further out, a series of colored acrylic panes caught the quickly fading sunlight and tossed it across the grass in brilliant reds, yellows, and blues.

I walked the gravel pathway, breathing deeply and feeling a calm settle onto my heart. Being outside was like balm for my weary mind. The buzz and rush of a hundred, tiny, ongoing responsibilities quieted as I sat on the shore of Lake Austin and gazed out across the water. Right here, I felt inspired to take a deep breath and count my blessings.

My life was beautiful. I had three wild and wonderful children who I adored. Their curiosity and imagination lit up my life. Dave was my solid foundation. He anchored me with his constant, unwavering love and support. I never felt alone in my concerns or challenges, because he bore life as an equal and encouraging partner. Our home was bright and filled with love. We were surrounded by friends that enriched our daily life. Having mountains of laundry to fold meant we had plenty of clothing, where so many go without.

I closed my eyes and sent a prayer heavenward. My head had cleared, my heart was filled to overflowing, and the challenges of the busy day had melted into appreciation for this moment. For this life. Through my rearview mirror on the drive home, I watched the sun cast rays of pink, purple, and orange, across the endless Texas sky. Taking a moment to get out of the house and reconnect with myself had been a good idea. In addition to all of my counted blessings, I was grateful for The Challenge that steered me to a place of real connection and inspiration rather than on a mood-boosting shopping trip. Because of that, I wasn't bringing home anything but an added measure of peace and contentment.

. . . . .

Retail therapy is the common practice of shopping in order to feel better. It is joked about in movies, offered as a suggestion between friends, and widely acknowledged as an effective way to get happier, fast. The little high from buying something new can momentarily boost your mood and make you temporarily happy, however the effects are short-lived.

The problem with retail therapy is that as soon as we bring home something new, it isn't new anymore and loses some of its luster. Buying things to feel better might offer a quick fix for a bad mood, but once those things are added to your closets and bookshelves, the effect wears off and you are left with less money and less space than you had before. Over time, retail therapy can contribute to growing discontent, debt, and stress because what you really want is to feel happy, not have more.

During The Challenge, I replaced retail therapy with self-care experiences that added to my well-being without adding to my piles of belongings. By not having the same get-happy-quick rush that retail therapy can provide, I had to get creative and find other ways to kick my occasionally grumpy self into gear. It took some experimenting, but soon enough I got into a groove.

Taking time to rest and recharge outside of hitting the mall became my new normal. I tried new restaurants, visited museums, went on hikes, took myself to the movies, and read good books while soaking in a bubble bath.

Some things, like walks in nature or taking long baths, didn't cost anything, and gave me even more space to think and relax than a shopping trip would have done. Some experiences that did cost money began to feel like an investment in my well-being and mental health. One simple example is getting a manicure.

I looked forward to my monthly nail appointments with eagerness. I kept my nails super short for crafting, but still always loved having them painted and looking nice. For years the idea of going to the nail salon seemed like a silly waste of money. I would rather spend my extra cash on things that "lasted," like clothing or tech.

Once we shut the door on buying those types of new items, I realized that I really enjoyed the experience of a manicure. Sitting quietly for an hour was a relief from the business of life, and since my hands were occupied, I couldn't even mindlessly scroll my phone. I started using my monthly nail appointments as a sort of meditation, using the time to close my eyes and ponder ideas, brainstorm projects, and fill myself with gratitude for the life I was living.

Choosing an experience that I enjoyed, that didn't offer something too tangible to add to my closet or cupboards, was a subtle change in the way I thought about spending money. Before The Challenge, I quantified good financial choices by the number and types of items I brought home. Now, I quantified them by the number and types of items I left in the store!

Not buying material goods as therapy meant leaving space open for reflection and peace in my home and life. Creating this kind of space in your own life might not come easily, or be. comfortable. It can feel isolating, scary, or even lonely to sit with yourself and be present with your emotions. In cases where someone spends most of their time alone anyway, this practice can feel redundant, but I believe the key is intention.

Spending time alone to scroll through my phone or meander a store meaninglessly, even if I wasn't buying things, was far less progressive toward the goal of learning and growing than spending time alone in a space where I was inspired, thoughtful, or grateful. As with most things, the more work we put in, the more benefit we can receive. Actively working on self-reflection and mindfulness practices in the place of mindless consumption brought a measurable added peace into my life.

. . . . .

Other mood-boosting habits started cropping up in my life, outside of taking time for myself. I realized that using what we have meant pulling things out of closets and drawers that I was saving for the perfect time to use them. We were living life right now. Now was the perfect time!

I started looking at my collection of nice candles differently. I loved the warmth and coziness of scented candles, so I continually bought them and tucked them away, not wanting to use them up. During The Challenge, I started pulling those candles out of the cabinet one by one, and burning them daily.

The soft glow and subtle smell brought me joy, and added a measure of calm to the house. I began lighting candles in the morning, near my computer when I was working, in the kitchen as I made dinner, and always while I took a bath. Instead of feeling like I was wasting the candles, I was intentionally burning them and enjoying every hour of flickering, lovely light.

. . . . .

Beyond solo time, manicures, and candles the most major replacement for retail therapy came in the form of simply understanding what I was really feeling when I needed to escape. Was there an actual problem that needed to be solved? Maybe a hard conversation I needed to have?

Being able to dig a little deeper than "I'm upset and shopping feels good," helped bring an added measure of intention to my relationship with myself. During The Challenge I began to be more open to uncomfortable feelings while I explored what I was really thinking about, or what story I was telling to create these emotions.

Sometimes, all I needed to feel better was to allow myself to understand why I was feeling frustrated, sad, overwhelmed, or misunderstood. When I could back up enough to recognize the thoughts that were causing my feelings, I could decide whether or not I wanted to believe them. Often, these reflections required some space to think, and so going on a walk in the park, taking a long bubble bath, or sitting at the nail salon helped create that space.

Other times, what I needed to really feel better was to get outside of myself and help someone else. I learned to be more aware of the needs of friends and neighbors. Baking a plate of cookies for someone who had just had surgery or calling a friend who I hadn't spoken to in a while spread good will and connection both to them and me. Tuning into what I was really feeling rather than trying to escape it, helped me determine what course of action might be best. More than any quick fix, this was a long-term lesson in self-awareness and true self care.

You probably relate to having an occasional hard day. Some days (and weeks and months) just don't go according to our plan. Maybe there is a more effective way to feel better than hitting the newest sale. If you find yourself shopping as an escape from challenges, relationship trouble, or uncomfortable emotions, I want to invite you to consider there may be a better way.

The rush of positive emotion that comes with retail therapy is temporary. When you get home and arrange your new things, often the high has already faded. Sometimes, it has even been replaced with buyer's remorse, or guilt. There is nothing inherently wrong with shopping, and in fact we do need wonderful, beautiful things that add value to our lives.

It is a better strategy for your mental health and well-being to buy those with intention when you recognize a need, rather than as a reaction to a circumstance you can't control.

When you use shopping as an excuse to boost your mood, the long-term effects are actually counterproductive. Adding unnecessary belongings to your life causes even more frustration. Depleting your bank account on meaningless stuff contributes to even more stress and anxiety about money. It is a very backwards approach to try to combat negative emotion with a behavior that can actually increase negative emotion.

. . . . .

Sometimes in life you will be uncomfortable, and that is okay. Sometimes you will have a hard day (or week or month). Bringing awareness to what you are feeling, and the thoughts that are behind those emotions, will allow you to begin stepping back into control of your own story. Negative emotions are as important as the positive ones. When you sit with them and understand why they are here, you will experience growth and strength.

Intentionally creating an environment that fosters positive emotion is an important strategy. What do you love that could help bring intention and joy more fully into your everyday life? Recognizing what you value, what you enjoy, and what you really need will encourage an environment of ongoing self care, rather than the short-lived and artificial spike of happiness that accompanies retail therapy.

20 REPLACEMENTS FOR RETAIL THERAPY

- ▷ Wander a museum
- ▷ Go to the movies
- ▷ Go on a walk
- ▷ Sit on the beach
- ▷ Visit a new restaurant
- ▷ Visit an old favorite restaurant
- ▷ Read a book
- ▷ Take a bath
- ▷ Write in a journal
- ▷ Make some art
- ▷ Call a friend
- ▷ Volunteer at a local charity
- ▷ Organize a closet
- ▷ Have your nails done
- ▷ Find a walking tour of your city
- ▷ Turn up the radio and take a scenic drive
- ▷ Hit the gym
- ▷ Take a class
- ▷ Visit the local library
- ▷ Lay in a hammock

"We pay for
things before,
during, and after
the moment we
purchase them.

Chapter 16

TIME AND ENERGY AS RESOURCES

fter dropping the kids off at school, I drove to the nearby grocery store and parked in the first row. It was a weekday, and the parking lot was mostly empty. "Not much shopping happens on a Wednesday at 10 a.m.," I thought.

I was familiar with this store. It was where I did most of our weekly grocery shopping, and where, before The Challenge, I had wandered the aisles when I wanted some distraction. Today, I was on a mission. I needed a bolt of white printer paper so I could finish printing some handouts for an upcoming workshop. Normally, my printer runs out of ink when I am halfway through a project. Today, it had run out of paper.

Even though I hadn't done any mindless browsing in the past several months, I remembered exactly where the office supplies were. I love office supplies, especially when they're cute. My home studio office had a drawer filled with useful, adorable items. Blush pink paper clips and brass scissors were as functional as they were joyful. I noted a darling brass stapler on the shelf as I turned into the office aisle. It would be a perfect match for my scissors. But not today.

Turning circles in the aisle, I looked for the printer paper and found it stacked between the manila envelopes and the packing bubble wrap. It was exactly where I expected it to be.

I grabbed a bolt, tucked it beneath my arm, and headed toward the checkout. I didn't have a cart or a basket, because I was only coming in for this one item. It fit easily beneath my elbow, and I barely noticed the flashes of seasonal decor displayed on every end cap as I made it back to the register and bought the paper.

This feeling was still new, even after months of not shopping. The feeling of lightness that came with knowing I didn't need anything beyond the consumable item I had come in for. Sometimes, I felt a little awkward as I left the store without even looking around to see the latest, shiny things for sale.

Before choosing not to shop for the year, every single trip into a store had included at least a short meander through the different sections. I remember distinctly asking myself how I would know whether or not I needed something else, unless I looked to see what was available! Now, that reasoning seemed very flawed. If I didn't know that I needed something, it was highly likely that I simply did not need it.

The time I spent wandering aimlessly in stores this year had dramatically decreased. It turned out that not needing to know what I may or may not need meant trips to the store were purposeful, simple, and quick. I had gained back that time and used it for pursuing new projects at home and in my business, spending time with my kids and husband, and doing other things that filled me up.

Within fifteen minutes from when I had parked, I was back in my minivan, belting along to Adelle, and on the road back to my house where I could finish printing my handouts.

. . . . .

I am not a productivity expert, but I can easily understand that when you stop spending time and energy on something, you automatically have more time and energy for other things. In our case, the pivot to only buying consumable goods during The Challenge meant I was no longer shopping (whether in the store or online) for whole categories of items. My time and energy skyrocketed as a result.

My list of to-do projects didn't get much shorter, but I accomplished a lot more of them. I found myself finally feeling like I had enough time to take a bath and read a book rather than spend an afternoon at the outlet mall. I was doing some of the things that I had always intended to do, but never seemed to make happen.

Unless you are an extremely schedule-conscious person, it is likely that you have very little idea how much time you actually spend shopping for things you don't need. And I consider energy an entirely separate resource. Both time and energy are valuable resources that impact our lives on a daily basis. Far too often, we trade them for activities and thoughts that don't add value or progress. We simply do what we have always done, or what we think we should do because that is what everyone else does.

The time involved with shopping goes way beyond actually buying. You spend time thinking about what to buy, then time researching where to buy it. You spend time driving to and from the store—or sometimes multiple stores. There is time involved with the actual walking through, picking up, trying on, evaluating, calling a friend from the dressing room for validation, and then buying.

But it doesn't stop there. Once you bring your new items home, you have to spend time putting them away. Then time washing and organizing them. There is a baseline maintenance that comes along with each new purchase. An unseen contract that binds us to months and sometimes years of upkeep and care. I wonder if the price tags listed "twenty-five dollars + three hours per year of washing, drying, folding, putting away, sorting, and organizing" how much more aware we would be of our purchases.

Beyond all of that, I have to address the time invested before you even shop. Do you consider the time that it took to make the dollars that you use on each of your purchases? How often do you think whether or not this purchase is worth an hour, or two, or a week, or a month of full-time hourly labor?

. . . . .

One day, when Dave and I were first married, I was at the mall with my oldest son, Milo. He was just a baby at the time, and I needed to just get out of the house for some sanity. I pushed the stroller into Anthropologie and steered him carefully between the racks of beautifully styled clothing. Even the displays in this store made my jaw drop and felt like works of art. Nearly everything was squarely outside of my allotted "play money" budget, but it was fun to just look.

When we reached the back corner of the store where shoes

were stacked on pale-colored boxes, I spotted a pair of olive green leather pumps that made my heart jump. They were beautiful. Soft, creamy leather with a gently gathered bow on the toe. I didn't wear high heels much, but these had solid, wide heels and when I slipped one onto my foot it felt sturdy. I could walk in these. I would love these.

I removed the shoe from my foot and flipped it over to see the price tag stuck to the sole. They were one hundred and twenty-eight dollars. Oof. I knew they would be expensive, but that was more than I expected. My mind immediately went to work thinking of how I could make this happen.

"If I sew one costume and sell it for fifty dollars, minus cost, I make about thirty dollars. So, by making five custom costumes I will have them all paid for. I can do that!" I thought. With the matter settled in my mind, I bought the shoes and happily left the store. Cooing a little bit to Milo as we continued on our way.

The next couple weeks were complete chaos. It was costume season, so I had plenty of opportunity to pick up side jobs. But what about my life? In buying those shoes, I had anchored myself to more than fifteen hours at the drafting table and sewing machine. That is without counting trips to the fabric store to pick up buttons and zippers and ribbon. Or considering trips to the post office to ship the costumes off to their owners.

I loved the work. It was creative and gratifying. And I literally spent fifteen hours of time I could have spent doing other things, working to buy one pair of shoes that I loved for a little while. If that price tag would have said "fifteen hours" instead of "one hundred and twenty-eight dollars" I might have reconsidered.

Now, I realize my hourly rate at that point in my hobby-sewing career was laughably low. If I had been working at a higher paying job, the hours counted towards paying for those shoes would have decreased in proportion. The point I invite you to consider is that we invest far more time into the things we buy than simply the time it takes to carry them from the rack to the checkout stand. We pay for them before, during, and after the moment we purchase them.

If we had that perspective as we considered what we really want to bring into our life, we may choose differently. When I stepped out of the routine of systematically buying things just because it was what I had always done, I realized how incredible it felt to be back in control of my own time. It was so amazing to reclaim this valuable resource that I hadn't even noticed I was piddling away on things that didn't make a lasting impact on my well-being, fulfillment, or joy. Also, only buying things when the budget allows and the money is available helps to avoid the anxiety and frustration that can come with consumer debt. It isn't always easy to not buy things that you can't afford, and instead exercise patience, wait, or recognize how you don't need it at all, but when you live within your means, you reserve so much time and energy by avoiding some of the negative emotions that can accompany overextending yourself.

. . . . .

What about energy? Even before we began The Challenge, I had started exploring the idea of energy as a resource. There were days when I put my kids down for naps, excited to get some alone time to accomplish something (anything!), before realizing I was so exhausted all I could do was take a nap myself. It dawned on me that I often had plenty of time. I was short on energy!

It had never really occurred to me before to manage my energy as well as my time. Creating a schedule, writing a to-do list, accomplishing tasks before a certain deadline—these were tactics I was familiar with. None of that scheduling mattered much if in the time I had allotted, I didn't have the energy necessary to complete my tasks. I needed to figure out how to use my energy levels as wisely as I did my hours.

This realization led me down a rabbit hole of self-reflection, online research, reading, and trying to discover how to better manage my energy. Through a year of trial and error, I focused on energy as a resource. I learned that my energy could be built up and sustained through doing things that I loved. Some activities, like exercise, would be physically draining, but contribute greatly to higher overall energy levels. Some simple activities, like mindlessly scrolling through Instagram, could be an instant energy drain if I wasn't careful about my intention.

Spending quality time engaged with my kids or husband boosted my energy. Multitasking often drained my energy, even though it offered a false sense of productivity. Being outside in the sunshine was an energy boost. Making decisions over and over again was an energy drain. Thoughts could build or drain my energy levels, depending on whether they were positive or negative.

Realizing how in control I was of my own energy levels, encouraged me to seek out activities and thoughts that built me up. I also learned to ignore activities or thoughts that drained my energy. One of the places where so much energy could be better managed was in the cycle of mindless consumerism and constant shopping.

Just like with time, the energy that is invested into shopping begins long before the purchase and continues after the items come home. You spend energy as you think about what to buy, and evaluate what items are just right. You spend energy worrying about whether or not you can afford things or whether or not they will live up to your expectations. You spend energy comparing your purchases to others. Comparing your life to others.

But it doesn't stop there. Once you bring your new items home, you spend energy feeling frustrated as you pick up the clutter from the floor every day. You spend energy feeling overwhelmed, or ungrateful. You may suffer from buyer's remorse and spend energy feeling guilty. It might also burn your energy to justify your purchases to your family or yourself.

So much of this investment of time and energy into our shopping is unnecessary because so many of the things we buy are unnecessary.

. . . . .

When we made the decision to press pause on the cycle of mindless consumption, we unknowingly accessed a new abundance of time and energy to spend in more meaningful ways. Slowly, at first, we noticed pockets of open time on the calendar and cushions of extra energy waiting in the wings.

A trip to the mall turned into a trip to the museum. Instead of walking away filled with stuff but empty of energy, I walked away filled with inspiration and empty of guilt.

An evening browsing and buying online turned into an evening cuddled on the couch, turning pages and whispering stories to my babies. Instead of mastering recent mark-downs, I was making real memories.

These tiny moments of trading the way things used to be for the way I wanted things to be added up quickly. After a couple months of The Challenge I could reflect back and see that our life was looking, and feeling, a lot more meaningful. After half the year, when we had to make the major decision about where to move and what changes we might make going forward, I could see that our life was better when we intentionally focused on spending time and energy on what mattered most. Things on that list included: meaningful work, impactful experiences, and each other.

TIME + ENERGY MANAGEMENT CHART

One of the best ways to begin choosing to use your time and energy with more intention is to realize how you are currently using it.

The following exercise will help you determine what you are spending your time and energy on now. At the end of the activity, I share a short quiz to help you determine some of the things in your life that build and drain your own energy levels.

DAILY/WEEKLY ACTIVIES

For one week, write down each of the activities you do, in one-hour increments. The more honest you are with yourself, the more useful this activity will be. By recording the time you spend on different activities, you will become more aware of the time that exists in your life and how to use it more intentionally.

DAILY/WEEKLY ENERGY

For one week, write down your perceived energy level on a scale of 1–10 in one-hour increments, along with any spark that you perceive may be possible for the increase or decrease. For example: 10 a.m., energy level 7, spark: working on creative project and feeling good! 4 p.m., energy level 3, spark: after-school lull, overwhelmed by the hours until bedtime.

	SUN	MON	TUE	WED	THU	FRI	SAT
8AM	ACTIVITY ENERGY SPARK						
9AM							
10AM							
11AM							
12PM							
1PM							
2PM							
3PM							
4PM							
5PM							
6PM							
7PM							
8PM							

"The Challenge had helped us change our mindset from following the path that had been readily trodden down before us, to intentionally choosing how we wanted to live, then forging our own path.

Chapter 17

A LIFE OF ADVENTURE

The sound of the helicopter blades whirred overhead. I caught a glimpse of my reflection in the floor-to-ceiling windshield of the aircraft. We were lifting straight off the ground next to Manawaiopuna Falls, the 400-foot-tall waterfall that had been made famous in the original Jurassic Park movie. When I watched that opening scene as a kid, I never imagined that I would be here.

Dave and I were flying next to the spraying water, turning circles so everyone caught the view of this magnificent place. Then the pilot left the falls in the distance and continued over the island, pointing out geographic features as we went.

The ground dropped away into a vast, red canyon. The Grand Canyon of the Pacific, known locally as Waimea Canyon, looked wild and mysterious from this vantage point. Misty white fog danced at the base of the cliffs, adding depth and beauty to the already stunning scene.

The canyon turned into beaches, and we flew out beyond the sand. With only turquoise blue waves beneath us, we began rounding the edge of the island towards the Na Pali coastline. Music pumping through my headphones built up the suspense, clearly orchestrated to add a dynamic dimension to this helicopter tour. Right at the apex of the symphony in my ears, the jagged spires of Na Pali burst into view. Vibrant green with tropical vegetation, these cliffs were nearly vertical. They sliced into the horizon without apology.

I beamed at Dave, who was sitting next to me in the front row of the helicopter. Being here, together, felt like a dream come true. We were living the life we wanted, right now. One year before, when we had celebrated our tenth anniversary, we had a lot of responsible excuses to not go on a big adventure. This year, things were different.

The seed for this eleventh anniversary trip to Kauai had been planted just weeks after we began The Challenge. I was at a conference in Palm Springs where I applied to a live pitch competition. The idea was that ten different bloggers would be given two minutes each to pitch a collaboration idea to a company. In this case, the company was Alaska Airlines, and the prize for winners was two round-trip tickets to anywhere they fly.

With nothing to lose, I applied for the competition and was thrilled when I was chosen to participate in the live pitching round. I had stood at the podium and explained to two hundred people and a row of Alaska Airlines Marketing Executives how our family had just embarked on a minimalist experiment for the year, because we believed that memories and experiences mattered so much more than things. I shared that through working with Alaska Airlines, I could spread this message of "Less Stuff, More Adventure™," by highlighting some of the adventures and fun times our family might have in locations where they fly.

I felt a buzz from head to toe when I was announced as one of the winning pitches. The team handed me an envelope with the airline vouchers, and told me they had connected with my message. It was relatable and a story they would like to share.

Minutes later I called Dave from the hallway and told him, "Babe, we're going on an anniversary adventure this year. Our commitment to not shopping has already manifested good luck and airline tickets! I can't wait to see what else we discover."

With our plane tickets to Kauai all settled, we went to work creating an itinerary filled with experiences we had always hoped for. We hiked to waterfalls and swung on rope swings into the rivers below. We ate açaí bowls topped with brightly colored tropical fruit every morning and watched the sky paint itself into a masterpiece at sunset every night.

Once we had seen the incredible Na Pali coastline from the hiking trail and the helicopter, we decided to add in a visit by sea, and booked a snorkel trip on a cruiser boat.

Dave and I dove down to see the fish up close, eyes wide with wonder. When we caught a glimpse of a green sea turtle calmly paddling through the water just feet below us I felt my heart catch in my throat. What was this life? How could we be so lucky? I was steeped in gratitude, joy, and love.

This trip felt like the culmination of our months of making new choices. We had woken up to our ability to choose what mattered most and disregard the rest. What we wanted was a life filled with gratitude, abundance, creativity, and adventure, and here we were living it.

· · · · ·

This year we had learned to lean into living life on our own terms. That had meant choosing a lot less stuff. We had chosen less new clothing and shoes, less new furniture and artwork.

Less technology, and less material gifts.

Even while we were wrapped up in choosing less, we had discovered so much more. We found more gratitude for what we already owned. We had developed more patience to wait for things we couldn't control. We had earned back time and energy to spend doing things we actually enjoyed. We had more money to spend on experiences, rather than things.

The Challenge had helped us change our mindset from following the path that had been readily trodden down before us, to intentionally choosing how we wanted to live, then forging our own path. When we decided what we wanted our life to look like, we realized we had everything we already needed, we just needed to shift a few priorities to align our experience more fully with what we believed.

I don't think that we realized what a dramatic shift in perspective would come from deciding to not buy non-consumable goods for a year. The changes in our mindset didn't only arise in direct relationship to not shopping, rather were subtle shifts as we dug into the idea of simply living a more intentional life.

During The Challenge we took the time to ask ourselves what we really wanted. Not just what seemed easy, or what was the next logical step in our path to success as an upper-middle-class millennial family living in suburban America. But, how did we want our life to feel? What did we want to experience? What did we believe was possible?

One of the themes that emerged quickly was that of adventure. Choosing to enjoy a bunch of new experiences hadn't been on our initial list of principles we wanted to develop during the year, but as we gained back time, energy, and money, our natural response was to get out and enjoy time together doing fun things!

After school we would play at parks and go out for ice cream. On weekends we had time to visit local museums, camp in nearby National Parks, and road-trip to visit family. I had always been a free spirit, but through the years had unknowingly traded in some of that freedom for a life that filled my time with responsibilities, cluttered our home with belongings, and committed our money to keeping up the race.

While we did find so much excitement and fulfillment in going on new adventures, we also discovered an equal amount of enjoyment in simply viewing our circumstances as an adventure, whatever they might be.

When Dave had to begin his new job a month before school ended in Texas and we already had a summer road trip planned, we decided it could be a grand adventure! I stayed behind and helped the kids finish school, sold the house, and said goodbye to our friends with the thought echoing through my mind: "This is all a new adventure!"

Dave started working his new job, and returned home at night to an air mattress in the bedroom of our recently rented and still empty tiny house in Virginia. He cooked dinner and ate it sitting on one kitchen chair, because our furniture, and his family, hadn't yet arrived. "This is all a big adventure!"

When the five of us were finally all together in Richmond, and the moving truck showed up to empty our belongings into the house, but they didn't all fit so they stacked boxes in the back yard and the front yard as if it were a giant yard sale, "What an adventure!" we thought. And then, when it rained on those stacked boxes, and piles of belongings were ruined in the rain, but we realized we really didn't need any of them anyway, it was all an adventure.

. . . . .

These types of experiences are not always those you might ask for, but by choosing to see them through the lens of an adventure, you automatically set yourself up for more happiness and adaptability than you might otherwise feel.

Adventure by its very nature means that something is about to happen and you don't know what it is or exactly how it's going to work out. Life is an adventure! You never really know what is about to happen.

Even with things you have planned down to the details, you don't know what all of the results will be. By being prepared with a mindset of adventure, you are able to feel peaceful, curious, and content as you navigate the circumstances of your life. You will feel more able to cope with unexpected changes along the way.

. . . . .

As I lived through all of the unexpected changes that came during The Challenge, I developed a theory about the types of principles that invited an adventure mindset. These ideas can be applied to taking a helicopter ride in Kauai, or taking your kids to the local playground. They can be applied to an unexpected move across town, starting a new job, or even seemingly negative events like lost luggage or a water pipe leak.

By focusing on developing an adventure mindset you will be more able to fully experience and even enjoy the unexpected.

EXPLORE

The first principle in an adventure mindset is to explore. You don't have to go very far to explore. You can explore ideas or concepts that you hadn't thought of. You could think of learning a new skill as an adventure rather than feeling down that you are not very good at it.

What happens when you explore? You are looking for things that you don't understand and learning about them. When you explore, you're tuned into the present moment. You're aware of your surroundings. You're looking for things that might be of interest and that might make an impact.

Being willing to explore means a submitting to the truth that you don't know everything. You don't already know what's going to happen or how everything is going to play out. Allow yourself to explore the circumstances of your life and you will be better prepared to approach them in a way that is fulfilling.

EXPERIENCE

The second principle in the adventure mindset is to actually experience the situation that you're going through. You don't experience things like that as a whole. You experience life moment by moment, hour by hour and day by day.

Keeping yourself present in the moment invites so much mindfulness and joy into life. You can be grateful in the middle of a challenge for one moment of peace or happiness. It is much easier to approach a situation minute by minute, hour by hour than it is to try to understand or process it as a whole. Try to stay present in your personal experiences.

ENJOY

The third principle is to enjoy what we are going through, even if it is not what we might have chosen. One way I like to encourage myself and my kids to enjoy unexpected or challenging situations is through adding something that we already know we love. Maybe that means playing your favorite music while you do endless piles of laundry, or pairing a trip to the dentist with the reward of visiting a friend on your way home. Being aware of what we love and can bring more abundance into our daily life increases our ability to enjoy the things we might not always choose.

ENTHUSIASM

My fourth principle for developing an adventure mindset is to be enthusiastic. Enthusiasm is simply positive energy. When you are enthusiastic, you bring positive energy to whatever circumstance you are facing and to people around you. You don't have to know, understand, or even like what you are facing in life to be able to bring enthusiasm to the table. That positive energy is built up inside yourself through your positive thoughts and emotions, and with intention, you can be enthusiastic about anything you go through.

ENTERPRISE

Finally, one of my favorite principles of adventure is enterprise. Enterprise is a word that means to be resourceful, innovative. It invites you to use your imagination and your ingenuity. Enterprise means to find creative solutions to whatever your problem might be. It turns you into a problem solver rather than a problem creator. When you exercise enterprise, you have a "make it work" attitude. You decide that no matter what comes your way, you will make the best of it.

. . . . .

This process of intentional, adventurous living invites you to stop simply walking the pathway that has been stomped out before you by the many and the masses. This is your chance to consider your own, unique, wild life and choose what you really want. And, beyond that, to choose every day how you want to feel within the circumstances of life that you simply cannot control.

A life of adventure is waiting just beyond you making the decision about what you want to do with your life. And then living it. The circumstances are all neutral. You get to choose how to move forward through the experiences of your life. You get to decide how to embrace a more meaningful, fulfilling, and sustainable lifestyle.

My hope is that after reading through these chapters and learning more about our experiences, you will recognize the same opportunity for adventure and abundance in your own life. You are surrounded by resources, choose to use them! You are filled with potential, choose to believe that!

Your life today, right now, is overflowing with hope and happiness that you can reach out and claim by shifting your perspective and leaning into gratitude, patience, and creativity. You already have, and are more than enough.

THE LIVE LIST ACTIVITY

As you finish this book, my hope is that you have had some ideas and insights about your own life. The value we found in not shopping went far beyond simply not buying things, but led us to a deeper understanding of what we really wanted to include in our experience as a family. We learned to consider what we want to do as well as how we want to feel.

Every day is an adventure, and so many circumstances are beyond your control. As you keep in mind the true values you want your life to reflect, you will be better able to navigate both the exciting and unexpected that comes your way.

The following exercise is designed to encourage reflection so you can start living the life you really want to lead.

VALUES

Use this space to brainstorm values that are meaningful to you. Examples might include: honesty, enthusiasm, humor, determination, patience, etc.

_____

_____

_____

_____

_____

_____

_____

_____

_____

_____

Looking at the above list, narrow down to your deepest, core values by crossing some off until you reach three to five.

Write down some examples of experiences or choices that invite these values into your everyday life.

_____

_____

_____

_____

_____

FEELINGS

Use this space to brainstorm some of the emotions that you want to experience on a regular basis in your life. Examples might include: joy, abundance, gratitude, courage, peace, etc.

_____

_____

_____

_____

_____

_____

_____

_____

_____

Write down some examples of experiences you have had in your life that invited these feelings.

_____

_____

_____

_____

EXPERIENCES

Use this space to brainstorm some experiences you would love to have in your life. Dream as big as you want to, there are no limits to your imagination. Examples may include traveling to Europe, growing a garden, performing in a local play, starting a business, running a marathon, etc.

_____

_____

_____

_____

_____

_____

_____

_____

Choose one of the items on your list to break down into action-able steps. What is the first action you can take to put yourself on a pathway towards that experience? Know that you don't have to have any of these experiences in order to feel the feelings you want in your life, or to live your core values. It sure is fun to have an adventure, though.

_____

_____

_____

_____

_____

_____

_____

EPILOGUE

'm sitting by a crackling fire in the lobby of a historic hotel in the Blue Ridge Mountains. This is the part of the book where I bring you up to speed on what happened after The Challenge. Once the ball dropped and our official year of The More Than Enough Stuff Challenge ended, what did we do? What have been the long-lasting effects of such a dynamic family experiment?

This, friends, is the most fun part. Looking back over The Challenge, and the year that followed, I can see clearly how our experiment planted seeds of intention that we will reap for years to come. We had no idea how fundamentally changed we would emerge.

One of the first indications of a deep perspective shift came in the first couple weeks of the new year. I processed the completion of the challenge by writing a blog post and sharing on my Instagram page (@livefreemiranda) that we had finished the year feeling amazing. The initial flood of response was "So, what was the first thing you bought?"

I didn't know how to answer. I didn't have a list, and hadn't bought anything yet, because I hadn't needed anything yet. There were lots of dingy, worn through clothing that would need replacing in time. But, there was also time. I wasn't in a hurry.

Well, actually, now that I think about it, we had bought something. Something major. On January 5th, 2018 we closed on a new house in Richmond, VA. We had spent six months living in 1000 square foot rental as we experimented with what type of a house and neighborhood we really wanted. I was excited about the idea of a fixer-upper, because I really enjoy renovation and design. And when I spotted a small, darling Cape Cod style home in a family-friendly neighborhood in the city, I knew it was meant to be ours.

We met for construction consultations during the holidays, then signed the papers and got to work. This home is 1400 square feet, with three bedrooms, two bathrooms, and a yard we can wrap our arms around.

For the first several months of the year after The Challenge, I designed, DIYed, and renovated the house with intention, thinking clearly about what our own, unique family needs were. I stayed focused on making a home for our own family, not one for anyone else.

In between house projects we continued to choose adventure

over things. Now, we shop when we need something, and choose what we buy with consideration. We naturally ask ourselves the questions: Will it be lasting, fulfilling, and matter? Does it add or take away from our family values? Will I throw it away next week or next month? Can we borrow one? Can we do without?

In addition to being intentional about our shopping, we have also continued to be intentional about the other ways we spend our time and resources. We traveled as a family, as a couple, and myself as an individual more in 2018 than ever before. In the spring we spent a week in Italy, which was our family Christmas gift of experience at the end of The Challenge. We also visited family and friends in San Francisco, and took a month-long road trip through Utah, Arizona, and Texas before the kids started school again.

We have truly simplified most areas in our life so we can focus on what matters most. I cook the same seven meals as a baseline every week. This frees up time, energy, and grocery budget for other things. I put together daily outfits from the same, small capsule style wardrobe that I have been using for years. And in 2018 Dave caught the simplified wardrobe bug, too. He didn't add clothing to his closet in 2017, but after The Challenge he was also able to let go and donate a bunch of old items he had, but never used.

I have been so motivated in the months following The Challenge to ensure I am using my time on the most impor-tant things. Much of my business has shifted from working so often with many different companies for sponsored blog posts to working more intentionally with just a few companies whose values align with my own. I also began traveling to teach creative workshops, launched a self-development and intentional living podcast (Live Free Creative) and designed a small line of products that encourage the lifestyle we love, "Less Stuff, More Adventure™." (shop.livefreecreative.co)

. . . . .

As a couple and a family we exercise regular reflection on what is happening in our daily life, what we want to happen, and how to close the gap. We have been better equipped to face challenges with gratitude and patience after spending so much time focusing on those skills and values, they have become second nature.

When our ceiling fell down weeks after we moved into the recently renovated house, we were glad no one was hurt and we had the means to repair it. A couple months later, when the entire house flooded due to an unexpected cleaning accident, we again felt deeply grateful for the silver linings. This was another adventure. This we could handle.

Our life is better in every way because of the choice we made to stop running the race long enough to make sure we were on the right road.

. . . . .

We are very much still taking steps along the journey to becoming just a little better each day. Perfection is not our goal, because perfection is a myth. Our movement forward involves a clear understanding that we already have everything we need to be as fulfilled today as we want to be. We know that we get to choose what we include in our life, from the material goods to the opportunities, to the thoughts that create our emotions.

We have learned, and understood, and begun to operate from a place of gratitude, patience, creativity, and abundance. We recognize we have more than enough. My hope is that within the experiences and exercises I have shared, you might realize that you do too.

ACKNOWLEDGMENTS

All my love and gratitude to my husband Dave, for his endless and consistent support and encouragement. He says "yes" to my ideas, shows up with midnight snacks for my late-night work sessions, and cares for our kids while I chase my dreams. Dave, you are truly both my anchor and the wind in my sails.

Hugs and high fives to my three brilliant kids, Milo, Eliot, and Plum for teaching me through their humble examples of finding joy in the simple moments of everyday life. You three light up my life and made both our minimalist challenge and this book an incredible adventure worth taking.

I'm grateful to my parents who encouraged confidence by teaching me to experiment, try again, and learn lessons for myself. To my in-laws who love unconditionally and are great examples of creating space and choosing what matters most.

A huge thank you to Morgan and the team at Firewire Creative for catching my vision of the design for this book, and bringing it to life so beautifully. And to my editor Stephanie for thoughtfully working with me to make my messages impactful.

Finally, sending all my love to the thousands of friends and fans who have shown up for me online and in real life as I have worked to build a community of confidence and creativity. There would be no books without readers, so thank you for being part of my journey.